Praise for *THE SOCIALIST*

"In *The Socialist Challenge Today*, Panitch, Gindin, and Maher address the most important and concrete questions that confront the socialist left today—questions concerning how to make sense of and navigate the simultaneous emergence of insurgent anti-neoliberal political expressions and an authoritarian neoliberalism that sometimes dresses up as populism. No one could be a better guide for us through these complex and contradictory issues, as their record of always grounded, always theoretically rich and deeply informed, and always strategically enlightening political analysis shows. Their work is to be treasured, and this book continues in that vein."

—Adolph Reed, Jr, professor emeritus
of political science, University of Pennsylvania

"This updated edition of *The Socialist Challenge Today* should be required reading for everyone on the left celebrating the return of socialist politics. If our enthusiasm is to generate lasting, structural change, we have to plan—how exactly do we get to where we want to go? We have to learn from the past, analyze the present, and anticipate the future with clear heads, sober senses, and relentless revolutionary optimism."

—Jodi Dean, author of *Comrade: An Essay on Political Belonging*

"This is the book we need at this moment of perilous uncertainty. Panitch and Gindin bring their formidable knowledge of the international left to bear as they scrutinize recent efforts at party building on the left. They provide us with some of the lessons, the guardrails, we need as we mobilize to overcome the dangerous, perhaps fatal, entanglements of late capitalism. So read this book, and join in the effort."

—Frances Fox Piven, author of *Challenging Authority:
How Ordinary People Change America*

THE SOCIALIST CHALLENGE TODAY

SYRIZA, CORBYN, SANDERS

LEO PANITCH and SAM GINDIN
With Stephen Maher

Revised, Updated, and Expanded Edition

Haymarket Books
Chicago, Illinois

Published in 2020 by
Haymarket Books
P.O. Box 180165
Chicago, IL 60618
773-583-7884
www.haymarketbooks.org
info@haymarketbooks.org

ISBN: 978-1-64259-128-6

Distributed to the trade in the US through Consortium Book Sales and Distribution (www.cbsd.com) and internationally through Ingram Publisher Services International (www.ingramcontent.com).

This book was published with the generous support of Lannan Foundation and Wallace Action Fund.

Special discounts are available for bulk purchases by organizations and institutions. Please email orders@haymarketbooks.org for more information.

Cover design by Rachel Cohen.

Printed in Canada by union labor.

Library of Congress Cataloging-in-Publication data is available.

10 9 8 7 6 5 4 3 2 1

CONTENTS

PREFACE TO THE SECOND EDITION

This little book, conceived in the context of the disappointments generated by the Syriza government in Greece so quickly after its election in 2015, addresses the challenges facing socialists today by analyzing in historical and theoretical perspective the limits and possibilities for class, party, and state transformation of the democratic socialist insurgencies inside the Labour Party in the United Kingdom and the Democratic Party in the United States. That the Syriza experience did not stifle these insurgencies at their birth indicated that the recent shift from protest to politics on the left was not ephemeral, but reflected both the depth of opposition to neoliberal austerity and a growing awareness of the importance of advancing radically ambitious policy agendas to overcome it.

Bernie Sanders's remarkable impact on the 2016 presidential primaries was followed by Jeremy Corbyn's leading the Labour party in 2017 to the largest increase in its vote since 1945. Both were the result of, and had a further effect of, reviving transformative socialist expectations on the left. Yet the Syriza experience had already served as a warning about how problematic a strategy of entering the state would be without adequate preparation for implementation of radical policies through structural changes in the state apparatuses and, even more problematic, without developing broad working-class capacities to fuel and sustain the shift from protest to politics at the base, especially in the face of the powerful forces that would have to be overcome.

How far there was still to go in both these respects was seen in the electoral defeat of Corbyn two years into the Brexit conjuncture of 2019, despite the popularity of the radical policies put forward in the most ambitious democratic socialist program anywhere since the 1970s. Whatever the outcome of the Sanders insurgency on the 2020 US election, we hope the historical and theoretical discussion as well as the analysis of contemporary developments undertaken here will be of use to all those engaged in the struggle for democratic socialism today.

The first edition of this book drew on our essay "Class, party and the challenge of state transformation" in the 2017 *Socialist Register*; this revised, updated and expanded second edition now also draws on the essay, 'Class politics, socialist policies, capitalist constraints', written with Stephen Maher, in the 2020 *Socialist Register*. For their help and encouragement on both editions of this book, we want wish to thank Tony Zurbrugg and Adrian Howe of Merlin Press in the United Kingdom, and John McDonald, Charlotte Heltai, and Lillian Duggan of Haymarket Books in the United States.

The analysis of contemporary developments offered here owes much to conversations with too many friends and comrades—a good number themselves political actors as well as observers in Greece, the United Kingdom, and the United States—to mention here. But, as we noted in the

acknowledgements to the first edition, we especially appreciate our interactions with Max Shanly in relation to following
developments in the Labour Party. We dedicate this book to
him as well as to his great political mentor, Tony Benn.

January 2020

1

THE REVIVAL OF
DEMOCRATIC SOCIALISM

One of the most unexpected aspects of the current political conjuncture has been the coming to the fore of socialists at the leadership levels of the British Labour Party and the US Democratic Party. Their class-focused political discourse, directed against the power of the capitalists, of the corporations, and of the banks—and the state policies and actions that reflect and sustain this power—no doubt speaks to many of the same popular discontents that have animated the rapid rise of explicitly populist xenophobic politicians on the right. But to dismiss those who advance today's socialist discourse as an equivalent left populism is mistaken in theory and misleading in practice. These socialist leaders are drawing fresh political attention to the dynamics, structures, inequalities, and contradictions of capitalism as the systemic core of neoliberal globalization and ruling class privilege and power.

It is significant that this new politics has galvanized tens of thousands of young people into groups like Momentum and the Democratic Socialists of America. Their affiliation thereby with the parties of the center-left is not only directly concerned with mobilizing support for these socialist leaders and their political discourse, but also using this support as a springboard for advancing class struggles in the workplace, the community, and the local state. Nothing like this has happened in at least three generations. The explosion of activist energy has much to do with the frustrations of two decades of episodic mass protests and the marginality of those small revolutionary groups, which themselves provided little strategic guidance beyond direct action—in both cases leaving to the side the matter of how to enter the state to change what it does, let alone to change what it is.

That this socialist resurgence should have happened in the UK and US, of all places, is remarkable. It reflects how deeply political parties are linked to states through electoral systems, which is itself an outcome of certain dialectical historical relationships between states and parties. The resolve, since the early 1980s, of the Members of Parliament belonging to the Socialist Campaign Group to remain inside the Labour Party—so fundamental to the propulsion of Jeremy Corbyn into the leadership—would never have happened without the barriers imposed by the "first-past-the-post" electoral system, with its bias against new parties, blocking any viable socialist alternative. Nor would the Independent Senator Bernie Sanders have contested for the Democratic Party presidential nomination, or socialists at other levels run on the Democratic Party ticket, except for the absence of proportional representation in US elections. On the other hand, the coalescing of socialist forces in recent years outside the mainstream center-left parties into new parties such as Die Linke in Germany, Syriza in Greece, Bloco de Esquerda in Portugal, and Podemos in Spain cannot be understood apart from the fact that openings for their entering the state are provided by electoral systems based on proportional representation.

Yet however thin and frayed the electoral base of the old center-left parties has become, including even the "classic" social democratic parties of Germany and Sweden, these parties remain the dominant partners in electoral and governmental coalitions that extend from the center left to the far left. This suggests that the mobilization of socialist support behind Corbyn and Sanders *inside* the dominant center-left parties may afford possibilities as radical, at least for the time being, as the mobilization of socialist electoral support outside these parties.

The renewed appeal of a socialist political discourse, one hundred years after the Russian Revolution and thirty years after its ignominious endpoint, has astonished the punditocracy. It does indeed appear that socialism in the twenty-first century has finally broken free of the Bolshevik legacy, which so defined—pro and con—the political discourse of the left throughout the twentieth century, often weighing "like a nightmare on the brains of the living." The emergence of a twenty-first century socialism that neither defines itself by the Bolshevik model, nor abjectly shrinks from advancing a socialist project for fear of being tainted by it, is itself a historic development. This is not to say that the Russian Revolution is forgotten, but only that, as young socialist activists mobilize against the timidity of career politicians and the machinations of the old center-left party and media establishment that keep them in place, such activists are today far more likely to be inspired by elements of its original revolutionary spirit than its specific revolutionary methods.

Yet the demise of the communist institutional tradition amid the survival of the social democratic one also carries with it a legacy that weighs on the brains of the living. This is seen in the tendency to clothe today's socialist agenda in the image of the policy achievements of the New Deal in the US and of postwar social democracy in Western Europe. The former largely ignores the compromises with capital that prevented the New Deal from ever turning into a social democratic welfare state, while the latter plays down how limited even postwar European social democracy was by its own explicit politics of class compromise. Foremost in mind on the left in recent decades is how far the US Democratic Party and the British Labour Party have traveled down the path to neoliberalism, while largely disregarded has been the fact that this was a common trajectory of all social democratic parties.

Indeed, despite the very different economic and social conditions today as compared with the postwar era, there is a tendency to present reforms in terms of merely picking up from 1935 or 1945. That said, there is a sharper awareness among socialists of how far the social democratic welfare state had, by the 1970s, already been beset by the contradictions of being married to the regeneration of a dynamic financial capitalism. Today's leadership of the Labour Party claims to inherit to the stifled Bennite agenda of the early

1970s, which was based on the recognition that it would be necessary to go beyond the postwar compromise with capital even to hold on to existing welfare state reforms. Yet the radical reforms advanced today, including the renationalization of the railways and other public utilities, fall far short of the pledge in *Labour's Programme for Britain 1973* to nationalize the twenty-five leading corporations across the key sectors of the economy alongside the planning agreements that other corporations would be tied to. Also notably absent is the 1976 Alternative Economic Strategy's focus on the need for import and capital controls.[1]

In contrast to the radical proposals for "taking capital away from capital" that emanated from within European social democratic parties in the 1970s—from the union-led socialization of the corporations in Sweden to the nationalization of the banks in France—the policies being advanced today by socialists inside the center-left parties look very modest. The emulation of the glory days of the New Deal or of postwar social democracy is inherently limited by the impossibility of restoring the particular social and economic conditions of those days. The past four decades of the internationalization of capitalist states—not least through the removal of capital controls and the free-trade agreements that codified their sponsorship of neoliberal globalization—have similarly rendered implausible any notion of merely rebooting the sti fled socialist agendas that emerged within social democratic parties at the height of the crisis of the Keynesian welfare state in the 1970s.

This makes it all the more imperative that socialists face squarely, and discuss far more openly than has yet been done, whether the policy proposals that are being advanced in the current conjuncture through an explicitly socialist discourse only amount to the revival of social democratic reformism, or foretell the emergence of a new strategy for structural reform that would create the conditions for taking capital away from capital. Any socialist-led government in the UK or US in the foreseeable future would have to face a still deeply integrated global capitalism, with capitalist-class economic dominance securely in place domestically, with working-class forces not strong enough, nor coherent enough, to sustain a full-blown challenge to that dominance, and with public institutions very far from having the capacity, let alone the orientation, to implement democratic economic and social planning.

Being in no position to take over the "commanding heights of the economy"—or even to introduce capital controls without immediately inducing more severe economic hardship than the austerity they are pledged to end—such a government would of necessity tread cautiously through piecemeal interventions against capitalist power and advance reforms that risk being overwhelmed in these conditions. All this would sustain the very significant oppositional elements inside the center-left parties at every level, and especially among the elected career politicians for whom a serious commitment to socialism, however gradualist, is regarded as a dangerous chimera. This poses the questions of how the socialist leadership of such a government could sustain its long-term ambitions, and what would distinguish its policies from the types of reforms advanced by progressive liberals and moderate social democrats today.

A first condition for building on electoral success would be to deliver some material gains for working people. In the context of the massive growth of inequality and high profits in both the UK and the US, there is in fact both the ideological and economic space for delivering improvements in people's lives through programs for social provision. A further step, which could open new paths to future structural reform, would be to expand economic democracy and public investment in infrastructure, transportation, and utilities. The crucial measure, however—one that distinguishes socialists from social democrats—is to develop these plans not in ways that would restore capitalist hegemony, but rather build the power, cohesion, and capacities of the working class to struggle for broader and deeper reforms than what are possible today. This would entail a systematic political education based on a sober acknowledgment of the barriers new socialist movements now face and what must be done to overcome them to realize that movement's larger potentials. But reforms and political education will not be enough. Significant gestures toward a post-capitalist future must be introduced and struggled over in the present. This requires a politics that is at every step engaged in directly confronting a profound dilemma: giant steps are impossible, yet small steps risk being swallowed into the logic of the system.

FROM SOCIAL DEMOCRACY TO DEMOCRATIC SOCIALISM

In 1917, not only those parties engaged in insurrectionary revolution but even those committed to gradual reform spoke of eventually transcending capitalism. Half a century later, social democrats explicitly came to define their political goals as compatible with a welfare-state variety of capitalism, and well before the end of the century, even many who had formerly embraced the legacy of 1917 would join them in this. Yet this shift occurred just as the universalization of neoliberalism rendered threadbare any notion of distinct varieties of capitalism. The realism without imagination of the Clinton-Blair "Third Way" was shown to ultimately lack realism as well as imagination.

However reactionary the era of neoliberal globalization has been, it has seemed to confirm the continuing revolutionary nature of the bourgeoisie, at least in terms of creating "a world after its own image."[2] Nevertheless, the financialized form of capitalism that greased the wheels not only of global investment and trade, but also of globally integrated production and consumption, was clearly crisis-prone.[3] The first global capitalist crisis of the twenty-first century, which began with the financial crash of 2007–08, was rooted in the contradictions attending the new credit-dependent forms through which, amid stagnant wages in the neoliberal era, mass consumption was sustained. Yet, in sharp contrast to the two great capitalist crises of the twentieth century in the 1930s and 1970s, as the crisis has unfolded over the past decade, it did not lead to a replacement of the regime of accumulation that gave rise to it. Unlike the move away from the Gold Standard regime in the 1930s and the abandonment of the Bretton Woods regime in the 1970s, the neoliberal regime persisted after 2008. Neoliberalism endured through the rescue and reproduction of financial capital, the reassertion of austerity in fiscal policy, the dependence on monetary policy for stimulus, and the further aggravation of income and wealth inequality—all of which were made possible by the continuing economic and political weaknesses of working classes everywhere through this period.

We are now at a new conjuncture. It is a very different conjuncture than the one that led to the perception that neoliberalism, at the height of its embrace by Third Way social democracy, was "the most successful ideology in world history."[4] While neoliberal economic practices have been reproduced—as has the US empire's centrality in global capitalism—neoliberalism's legitimacy has been undermined. The aftershocks of the US financial crash of 2008 reverberated across the eurozone and the so-called BRICS (Brazil, Russia, India, China, South Africa), deepening the multiple economic, ecological, and migratory crises that characterized the following decade. At the same time, neoliberalism's ideological delegitimization has enveloped many political institutions that have sustained its practices, from those of the European Union to political parties at the national level. What makes the current moment so dangerous is the space this ideological crisis has opened for the far right, with its ultranationalist, racist, sexist, and homophobic overtones, to capture popular frustrations with liberal democratic politics.

The recent delegitimization of neoliberalism has restored some credibility to the radical socialist case for transcending capitalism as necessary to realize the collective, democratic, egalitarian, and ecological aspirations of humanity. It has spawned a growing sense that capitalism can no longer continue to be bracketed when protesting the multiple oppressions and ecological threats of our time. And as austerity took top billing over free trade, the spirit of anti-neoliberal protest also shifted: whereas capitalist globalization had defined the primary focus of oppositional forces in the first decade of the new millennium, the second decade opened with the Occupy movement in the US and the *Indignados* anti-austerity movement in Spain dramatically highlighting capitalism's gross class inequalities. Yet with this shift, the insurrectionary flavor of protest without revolutionary effect quickly revealed the limits of forever standing outside the state.

The marked turn on the left from protest to politics that has come to characterize the new conjuncture, as opposition to capitalist globalization shifted from the streets to the state theaters of neoliberal practice, was in good part what the election of Syriza in Greece and the sudden emergence of Podemos in Spain signified. Corbyn's election as leader of the British Labour Party attracted hundreds of thousands of new members with the promise to sustain activism rather than undermine it. And even in the US, the heartland of the global capitalist empire,

only a short bridge spanned Occupy and Sanders's left populist promise for a political revolution "to create a government
which represents all Americans, and not just the 1 percent."
This was reflected in polls indicating that half of all millennials
did not support "capitalism" and held a positive view of "socialism"—whatever they thought those terms meant.

This transition from protest to politics has been remarkably
class-oriented in terms of addressing inequality in income
and wealth distribution, as well as in economic and political power relations. Yet as Andrew Murray has so incisively
noted, "this new politics is generally more class-focused than
class-rooted. While it places issues of social inequality and
global economic power front and center, it neither emerg-
es from the organic institutions of the class-in-itself nor ad-
vances the socialist perspective of the class-for itself."[5] The
disappointment that trade unions so often experience with
the center-left parties whose base they form actually reflects
the loss of these parties' class focus once they are elected as
they turn to govern in the "national interest." But the larger
strategic question pertains to how a class-rooted politics—in
the original sense of the connection between working class
formation and political organization—could become transformative today. What could the manifold changes in class
composition and identity, as well as the limits and failures of
traditional working-class parties and unions in light of these
changes, mean in terms of new organizational forms and
practices? And what would a class-focused and class-rooted
transformation of the capitalist state entail?

While leaders like Tsipras, Iglesias, Corbyn, and Sanders all have pointed beyond Third Way social democracy, their capacity to move beyond it is another matter. This partly has to do with their personal limitations, but much more with the specific limitations of each of their political parties, including even the strongest left currents within them, and their failure to prepare adequately for the challenge of transforming state apparatuses. The experience of the government in Greece highlights this shortcoming, as well as how difficult it is for governments to extricate their state apparatuses from transnational ones.

All these factors compel a fundamental rethink of the relationship between class, party, and state transformation. If Bolshevik revolutionary discourse seems archaic a hundred years after 1917, it is not just because the legacy of its historic demonstration that revolution was possible has faded. It is also because the impossibility of an insurrectionary path to power in states deeply embedded in capitalist societies—as Gramsci clearly explained so soon after 1917—remains as real as ever. What this means for socialists, however, as we face up to a long war of position in the twenty-first century, is not only the recognition of the limitations of twentieth-century Leninism, let alone Soviet state practices. It also entails an appreciation of what inspired the communist break with social democracy in the first place—what Jodi Dean admires today as communism's expression of the "collective desire for collectivity."[6] It also requires a commitment to working-class internationalism as opposed to national class harmony between capital and labor, an orientation to class formation and organization in the struggle against capital, and a recognition that socialist economic planning requires taking capital away from capital.

Democratic socialism in the twenty-first century must encompass all that was positive about the communist vision even while negating twentieth-century Communist Party and state practices by virtue of an indelible commitment to developing democratic capacities to the end of democratizing the economy and the state. This is crucial for retaining a clear distinction between democratic socialism and social democracy. Indeed, given the latter's own history of incorporation into the capitalist state and embrace of neoliberalism, engaging successfully in the long war of position in the twenty-first century will above all require discovering how to avoid the social democratization of those now committed to transcending capitalism. This is the central challenge for socialists today.

2

CLASS, PARTY, STATE: THE TWENTIETH-CENTURY SOCIALIST EXPERIENCE

The *Communist Manifesto* of 1848 introduced a new theory of revolution. Against the conspiracies of the few and the experiments of the dreamers, an emerging proletariat was heralded with the potential to usher in a new world. The argument was not that these dispossessed laborers carried revolution in their genes; rather, it pointed to their potential for organization, which was facilitated by modern means of communication as well as by the way capitalists collectivized labor. Even though their organization would be "disrupted time and again by competition amongst the workers themselves," it indeed proved to be the case that "the ever expanding union of the workers" would lead to "the organization of workers into a class, and consequently into a political party."[1]

It was this sense of class formation as process that led E.P. Thompson to argue so powerfully that class was not a static social category but a changing social relationship, which historically took shape in the form of class struggle before class. Out of the struggles of the dispossessed laborers against the new capitalist order in England in the last half of the eighteenth century and the first half of the nineteenth came the growing collective identity and community of the working class as a social force.[2] Moreover, as Hobsbawm subsequently emphasized, it was really only in the years from 1870 to 1914—as proletarianization reached a critical mass, and as workers' organizational presence developed on a national and international scale through mass socialist parties and unions—that the revolutionary potential in the working class that Marx had identified looked set to be realized.[3] However arcane the very term "workers' state' may now seem, it made sense to people in 1917—and not least to nervous bourgeoisies.

Yet there was much that made all this problematic even then. The fact that so many trade unions had emerged that had nothing to do with socialism reflected how far even the newly organized industrial proletariat stood from revolutionary ambitions. And where there was a commitment to socialist purposes, as was ostensibly the case with the social democratic parties of the Second International, it was compromised in serious ways. The winning of workers' full franchise rights had the contradictory effect of integrating them into the nation state, while the growing separation of leaders from members inside workers' organizations undermined not only accountability, but also the capacity to develop workers' transformative potentials. This was of course contested in these organizations even before Roberto Michels outlined their oligarchic tendencies in his famous book.[4] But these two factors—a class-inclusive nationalism and a non-transformative relationship between leaders and members in class organizations—combined to determine why the catastrophic outcome of inter-imperial rivalry announced with the guns of August 1914, far from bringing about the international proletarian revolution, rather ambushed European social democracy into joining the great patriotic war and making truce in the domestic class struggle.

What made the idea of proletarian revolution ushering in a workers' state still credible after this—perhaps all the more credible—was the Russian Revolution. But what Rosa Luxemburg discerned within its first year would definitively mark the outcome: a revolutionary process that, in breaking with liberal democracy, quickly narrowed rather than broadened the scope of public participation, ending as a "clique affair." Lenin, she noted, saw the capitalist state as "an instrument of oppression of the working class; the socialist state, of the bourgeoisie," but this "misses the most essential thing: bourgeois class rule has no need of the political training and education of the entire mass of the people, at least not beyond certain narrow limits." The great danger was that

> without general elections, without unrestricted freedom of press and assembly, without a free struggle of opinion, life dies out in every public institution, becomes a mere semblance of life, in which only the bureaucracy remains as the active element. Public life gradually falls asleep, a few dozen party leaders of inexhaustible energy and boundless experience direct and rule. Among them, in reality only a dozen outstanding heads do the leading

and an elite of the working class is invited from time to
time to meetings where they are to applaud the speeches
of the leaders, and to approve proposed resolutions unan-
imously—at bottom then, a clique affair.[5]

Isaac Deutscher, looking back some three decades later, suc-
cinctly captured the dilemma that had led the Bolsheviks to
bring about a dictatorship that would "at best represent the
idea of the class, not the class itself." He insisted that, in consolidating the new regime, the Bolsheviks had not "clung
to power for its own sake," but rather had reflected a deeper quandary. Even though anarcho-syndicalists seemed "far
more popular among the working class," the fact that they
"possessed no positive political programme, no serious organization, national or even local" only reinforced the Bolsheviks' identification of the new republic's fate with their own,
as "the only force capable of safeguarding the revolution":

> Lenin's party refused to allow the famished and emotion-
> ally unhinged country to vote their party out of power
> and itself into a bloody chaos. For this strange sequel to
> their victory the Bolsheviks were mentally quite unpre-
> pared. They had always tacitly assumed that the majority
> of the working class, having backed them in the revolu-
> tion, would go on to support them unswervingly until
> they had carried out the full programme of socialism.
> Naive as the assumption was, it sprang from the notion
> that socialism was the proletarian idea par excellence and
> that the proletariat, having once adhered to it, would not
> abandon it .... It had never occurred to Marxists to reflect

whether it was possible or admissible to try to establish socialism regardless of the will of the working class.[6]

The long-term effects of what Luxemburg had so quickly understood would contribute to reproducing a dictatorial regime regardless of the will of the working class—and, relatedly, also to the gaps in the "political training and education of the entire mass of the people"—were chillingly captured by what a leader of the local trade union committee at the Volga Automobile Plant (AVTOVAZ) said to us in an interview in 1990 just before the regime established in 1917 collapsed: "Insofar as workers were backward and underdeveloped, this is because there has in fact been no real political education since 1924. The workers were made fools of by the party."[7] The words here need to be taken literally: the workers were not merely fooled, but *made* into fools; their revolutionary understanding and capacity was undermined.

The fillip that 1917 had given to fueling workers' revolutionary ambitions worldwide was more than offset by the failure of the revolution in Germany and the Stalinist response to an isolated and beleaguered Soviet Union after Lenin's death, with all the adverse consequences both entailed. Though the specter of Bolshevism hardly faded, it was the specter of fascism that dominated radical change in the interwar years. Nevertheless, there was also widespread recognition of the potential of the working class as the social force most capable of transforming state and society. This perception was not least based on worker organization and class formation during the Great Depression in the US, which was already by then the new world center of capitalism. Leading American capitalists and state officials believed as they entered World War II that, among the barriers to the remaking of a liberal capitalist international order, "the uprising of [the] international proletariat . . . [was] the most significant fact of the last twenty years."[8]

The strength of the organized working class as it had formed up to the 1950s was registered in the institutionalization of collective bargaining and welfare reforms. The effects of this were highly contradictory. The material gains in terms of individual and family consumption, which workers secured directly or indirectly from collective bargaining for rising wages as well as from a social wage largely designed to secure and supplement that consumption, were purchased at the cost of union and party practices that attenuated working class identity and community—especially in light of the restructuring of employment, residency, and education that accompanied these developments. To be sure, the continuing salience of working-class organization was palpable. This was increasingly so in the public sector, but it was also measurable in class struggles in the private sector, which resisted workplace restructuring, as well as in the wage-led inflation that contributed to the capitalist profitability crisis of the 1970s. Yet the failure to renew and extend working-class identity and community through these struggles opened the way to the neoliberal resolution of the crises of the 1970s through a widespread assault on trade unionism and the welfare state, and the interpellation of workers themselves as "taxpayers."

SIGNPOSTS TOWARD DEMOCRATIC SOCIALISM

It was the exhaustion of both social democratic and communist parties as agents of social transformation that in good part fueled the radicalism of the New Left in the 1960s. Although the student radicalism and industrial militancy of the late 1960s led to a sharp turn by activists to extra-parliamentary forms of activity, the reverberations were bound to be felt in the parties as well. This entailed, first of all, a revival of a democratic socialist discourse in party debates. In particular, the language of "class," of "movement," of "capital," of "exploitation," of "crisis," of "struggle," of "imperialism," even of "transformation," while never entirely extirpated from social democratic parties, had certainly become marginalized within them in the decades after World War II. But by the early 1970s, all such terminology was again within constant earshot at party meetings and conferences. Even the term "social democracy" had often been used pejoratively, yet many of the most jaded leaders were now calling themselves "democratic socialists."

But more than language was involved in this revival: there was a programmatic turn as well, whereby the questions of taking capital away from capital through major extensions of public or workers' ownership (or at least through radical measures of investment planning and industrial democracy) and the pursuit of a foreign policy independent of the United States, came onto the agendas of some of these parties. Certainly only the most naive observer or participant could have thought in the 1970s that these parties had actually been transformed into effective vehicles for a socialist transition; the more cynical remained convinced that they were in the process of reconstructing their viability as mediating agencies for the consensual reproduction of capitalism and the containment of industrial militancy and radical structural reform. Nonetheless, the new discourse and programmatic thrust did carry with it an explicit critique of established social democratic practice.

The question remained, of course, whether socialism could be placed back on the agenda, not only of these parties, but in the broader political arena. It certainly cannot be claimed that there was a ready-made groundswell of socialist electoral opinion just waiting to be tapped: it needed to be created in the interplay between party discourse and popular experience. The eventual victories in the early 1980s of the French, Greek, and Swedish parties on the basis of the most radical programs put before their electorates at least since the 1940s certainly invalidated simplistic claims that parties that advanced such a program were inherently unelectable. Yet if a socialist alternative was to not only avoid conjuring up a negative electoral reaction, but to produce the popular support needed to sustain a socialist government's radical thrust, a sea change in the organizational and ideological practices of parliamentary socialist parties themselves needed to take

place. They had to become unified around the socialist alternative; they had to find the means to be effective vehicles
for a transformation and mobilization of popular attitudes;
they had to develop mechanisms to ensure that their leader-
ships not only mouthed a socialist discourse that the activists
wanted to hear at party meetings, but shared a commitment
to radical change and maintained such a commitment even
once subject to the conservatizing pressures of office.

It was a tall order indeed. The programmatic changes
that occurred in a number of social democratic parties in
the 1970s were obviously developed with some awareness of
these questions, as in the emphasis placed on industrial democracy alongside nationalization and investment controls,
or on the decentralized socialization of capital through trade
union and community-administered wage-earners' funds.
These policies were conceived with a view to popularizing
a socialist alternative via obviating its association with the
authoritarian practices of Eastern European "actually existing socialisms" as well as the bureaucratic practices of state-
owned enterprises in the West. But this attempt at renewal
was itself a small first step. For even to make this endeavor
credible and popular, fundamental organizational changes
within the social democratic parties themselves were necessary to make them effective vehicles for a democratic socialist
alternative.

In every case the established forces in these parties succeeded in repelling this challenge. In some cases this happened quickly, as with the expulsion in the early 1970s of

both the Young Socialists from the German SPD and the Movement for an Independent Socialist Canada from the New Democratic Party. In other cases, it took over a decade, as in the watering down of the Meidner Plan for socializing capital in Sweden through wage-earner ownership funds, or the U-turn of the Mitterand government in the early 1980s in France. The most promising and most protracted intraparty struggle occurred in the British Labour Party around the Alternative Economic Strategy and the Campaign for Labour Party Democracy running through the 1970s until the defeat of the Bennite insurgency in the early 1980s by a coalition of old left parliamentarians and union leaders.[9]

These intraparty struggles, including those between the Eurocommunists and the old guard in the communist parties, stimulated a much broader discussion on the European left, represented by Gorz, Magri, Benn, Miliband, Poulantzas, Rowbotham, Segal, and Wainwright among others, oriented to discovering new strategic directions. They pointed beyond both the Leninist and social democratic "models," which, despite taking different routes, nevertheless evinced in their practices a common distrust of popular capacities to democratize state structures.[10]

This new direction was especially well articulated in Poulantzas's "Toward a Democratic Socialism"[11]: "There is no longer a question of building 'models' of any kind whatsoever. All that is involved is a set of signposts which, drawing lessons of the past, point out the traps to anyone wishing to avoid certain well-known destinations," not least the "techno-bureaucratic statism of the experts." These traps were the outcome not only of the instrumentalist strategic conception of social democratic parliamentarism, but also of the "Leninist dual-power type of strategy which envisages straightforward replacement of the state apparatus with an apparatus of councils." In both cases,

> [t]ransformation of the state apparatus does not really en-ter into the matter. First of all the existing state power is taken and then another is put in its place. This view of things can no longer be accepted. If taking power denotes a shift in the relationship of forces within the state, and if it is recognized that this will involve a long process of change, then the seizure of state power will entail con-comitant transformations of its apparatuses . . . . In aban-doning the dual-power strategy, we do not throw over-board, but pose in a different fashion, the question of the state's materiality as a specific apparatus.

Notably, Poulantzas went back to Luxemburg's critique of Lenin in 1918 to stress the importance of socialists building on liberal democracy, even while transcending it, in order to provide the space for mass struggles to unfold that could "modify the relationship of forces within the state appara-tuses, themselves the strategic site of political struggle." The very notion *to take* state power "clearly lacks the strategic vision of a process of transition to socialism—that is of a long stage during which the masses will act to conquer power and transform state apparatuses." For the working class to displace the old ruling class, in other words, it must develop capacities to democratize the state, which must always rest on "increased intervention of the popular masses in the state . . . certainly through their trade union and political forms of representation, but also through their own initiatives within the state itself." To expect that institutions of direct democracy outside the state can simply displace the old state in a single revolutionary rupture in fact avoided all the difficult questions of political representation in the transition to and under socialism.

Indeed, as André Gorz had already insisted in his path-breaking essay "Reform and Revolution" a decade earlier, taking off from liberal democracy on "the peaceful road to socialism" was not a matter of adopting "an a priori option for gradualism; nor of an a priori refusal of violent revolution or armed insurrection. It is a consequence of the latter's actual impossibility in the European context."[12] The advancement of what Gorz called a "socialist strategy of progressive reforms" did not mean the "installation of islands of socialism in a capitalist ocean." Rather it involved the types of "structural reforms" or "non-reformist reforms" that could not be institutionalized so as to close off class antagonism but that allowed for further challenges to the balance of power and logic of capitalism, thereby introducing a dynamic that allowed the process to go further. In calling for the creation of new "centres of social control and direct democracy" outside the state, Gorz was farsighted in terms of the contributions such centers could make to a broad process of new class formation with transformative potential, not least by extending to "the labour of ideological research" and more generally to the transformative capacities of "cultural labour aiming at the overthrow of norms and schemata of social consciousness." This would be essential for ensuring that "the revolutionary movement's capacity for action and hegemony is enriched and confirmed by its capacity to inspire ... the autonomous activity of town planners, architects, doctors, teachers, and psychologists."[13]

What Gorz's formulation left aside, however, were the crucial changes in state structures that would need to attend this process. Poulantzas went to the heart of the matter, a decade later, stressing that on "the democratic road to socialism, the long process of taking power essentially consists in the spreading, development, coordination, and direction of those diffuse centres of resistance which the masses always possess within the state networks, in such a way that they become real centres of power on the strategic terrain of the state." Even Gramsci, as Poulantzas pointed out, "was unable to pose the problem in all its amplitude" since his "war of position" was conceived as the application of Lenin's model/strategy to the "different concrete conditions of the West" without actually addressing how to change state apparatuses.[14] Yet it must also be said that Poulantzas, even while highlighting the need for taking up the challenge of state transformation, did not himself get very far in detailing what changing the materiality of state apparatuses would entail in specific instances. Lurking here was the theoretical problem

Miliband had identified of not differentiating state power from class power, and therefore not specifying sufficiently how the modalities and capacities involved in exercising capitalist state power would be changed into different modalities with structurally transformative capacities.[15] And as Göran Therborn pointed out, in envisaging an important role for unions of state employees in the process of transforming state apparatuses, it was necessary to address the problem that "state bureaucrats and managers will not thereby disappear, and problems of popular control will remain," thus continuing to pose "serious and complicated questions" around the transformation of the state through socialist democracy.[16]

Socialists have since paid far too little attention to the challenges this poses.[17] There was a growing recognition that both insurrectionary politics to "smash the state" and the social democratic gradualism were dead ends. At the same time, this recognition was accompanied by a penchant for developing "market socialist" models in the late 1980s, which has subsequently been succeeded by the creation of a spate of radical left literature that—in almost a mirror image of neoliberalism's championing of private corporations and small business firms against the state—weakly points to examples of cooperatives and self-managed enterprises as directly bearing socialist potential.[18] Replicated here is exactly what Poulantzas identified in the conception of those for whom "the only way to avoid statism is to place oneself outside the state. The way forward would then be, without going as far as dual power, simply to block the path of the state from the outside."

Yet by concentrating exclusively on "breaking power up and scattering it among an infinity of micro-powers," the result is that the "movement is prevented from intervening in actual transformations of the state, and the two processes are simply kept running along parallel lines."[19]

3

FROM PROTEST TO PARTY TO STATE: LESSONS FROM SYRIZA

The only party to the left of traditional social democracy in Europe that succeeded in winning a national election since the current economic crisis began was Syriza in Greece. Syriza's roots go back to the formation of Synaspismos, first as an electoral alliance in the 1980s, and then as an independent, although factionalized, new party in the early 1990s. This was part of the broader institutional reconfiguration inaugurated by the Eurocommunist strategic orientation, searching for a way forward in the face of communist as well as social democratic parties having lost their historic roles and capacities as agencies of working-class political representation and social transformation. This search went all the way back to the 1960s and accelerated after the collapse of the Soviet bloc and social democracy's embrace of the Third Way. In Greece especially the Eurocommunist orientation was characterized by continuing to embrace the tradition of political revolution as experienced in the Civil War after 1945, even while distancing itself from the Soviet regime; and it would increasingly be characterized by the inspiration it took from, and a willingness to work with, new social movements.

Through the 1990s Synaspismos offered enthusiastic support for European integration, but as the neoliberal form of the Economic and Monetary Union buried the promises of a European social charter, the grounds were laid in Greece, as elsewhere on the European radical left, for a more "Euroskeptical" orientation.[1] This new critical posture toward the European variety of capitalism was a crucial element in Synaspismos explicitly defining, by the turn of the millennium, its strategic goal as "the socialist transformation of Greek society" while increasingly encouraging "dialogue and common actions" not only with the alter-globalization movement, but with radical ecologists and political groups of a Trotskyist or Maoist lineage. The Coalition of the Radical Left, with the acronym Syriza, emerged out of this with the goal, as Michalis Spourdalakis put it, "not so much to unify but rather to connect in a flexible fashion the diverse actions, initiatives, and movements . . . and to concern itself with developing popular political capacities as much as with changing state policy." But turning Synaspismos, and through it Syriza, into such a party was, as Spourdalakis immediately adds, "more wishful thinking than realistic prospect."[2]

As the euro crisis broke, however, with Greece at the epicenter of the attempt to save the euro through the application of severe austerity, all the elements of Syriza threw themselves into the 2011 wave of protests, occupations, and strikes, while supporting the four hundred or so community solidarity networks around the country to help the worst affected cope. This prepared the ground for Syriza's electoral breakthrough of 2012. Syriza's active insertion into the massive outbursts of social protest across Greece the year before was a source of radical democratic energy that went far beyond what can be generated during an election campaign, however successful. The importance of sustaining such energy was eloquently articulated at Syriza's Congress in 2013, when it finally turned itself from an electoral alliance into a single-party political organization. The conclusion to its founding political resolution called for "something more" than the programmatic framework that resolution set out. Since "for a Government of the Left, a parliamentary majority—whatever its size—is not enough," it called for "the creation and expression of the widest possible, militant and catalytic political movement of multidimensional subversion":

> Only such a movement can lead to a Government of the Left and only such a movement can safeguard the course of such a government ... [that] carries out radical reforms, takes on development initiatives and other initiatives of a clear environmental and class orientation, opens up new potentials and opportunities for popular intervention, [and] helps the creation of new forms of popular expression and claims . . . . Syriza has shouldered the responsibility to contribute decisively to the shaping of this great movement of democratic subversion that will lead the country to a new popular, democratic, and radical changeover.[3]

This sort of language, articulating this sort of understanding, was rare on the European radical left, let alone anywhere else. Yet as the Syriza leadership contemplated the dilemmas it faced as it stood on the doorstep of government, its concern to appear as a viable government in the media's eyes led it to concentrate, as was evident in the Thessaloniki Programme proclaimed just a year later, on refining and scaling down the policy proposals in the 2013 party program. This was done with little internal party consultation, with the leadership mainly concerned with there not being enough experienced and efficient personnel in the party to bring into the state to change the notoriously clientelistic and corrupt state apparatus. Little attention was paid to who would be left in the party to act as an organizing cadre in society. The increase in party membership was not at all proportionate to the extent of the electoral breakthrough. Even when new radical activists did join, the leadership generally did very little to support those in the party apparatus who wanted to develop these activists' capacities to turn party branches into centers of working-class life and strategically engage with them, preferably in conjunction with the solidarity networks, in planning for alternative forms of production and consumption. All this spoke to how far Syriza still was from having discovered how to escape the limits of social democracy.

SYRIZA AND THE PROBLEM OF
STATE TRANSFORMATION

Within a month of Syriza's election at the end of January 2015, Stathis Kouvelakis, a member of Syriza's Central

Committee whose interpretation of the dramatic unfolding of events in his country garnered widespread attention, urged the international left to regard soberly the limits of what the new government could accomplish. In a debate with Alex Callinicos in London on February 25, Kouvelakis addressed the disappointments already felt when the new government agreed to renew negotiations with the EU and IMF:

> [This] is not a "betrayal." It's not about the well-known scenario "they have sold out." We have seen that there was real confrontation. We have seen the amount of pressure, the blackmailing by the European Central Bank. We have seen that they want to bring the Syriza government to its knees. And they need to do that because it represents a real threat, not some kind of illusion of a reformist type. So the reality is that the representatives of the Greek government did the best they could. But they did it within the wrong framework and with the wrong strategy and, in this sense, the outcome couldn't have been different. . . . The people who think that "the reformists will fail" and that somehow in the wings stands the revolutionary vanguard who is waiting to take over somehow and lead the masses to a victory are I think completely outside of reality.[4]

Less than five months later, as these negotiations infamously came to a climax, Kouvelakis, along with many others, would leave Syriza in response to what he now called the government's "capitulation," which indeed became the most common epithet used by the international left. Yet the need to ask whether the outcome could really have been different was now greater than ever. And while the answer did indeed hinge on the adequacy of Syriza's strategy in relation to Europe, that in turn related to deeper issues of party organization, capacity building, and state transformation—as well as the adequacy of strategies on the wider European left, at least in terms of shifting the overall balance of forces.

The common criticism of Syriza, strongly advanced by the Left Platform group in the party, was that it had not developed a "Plan B" for leaving the eurozone and adopting an alternate currency as the key condition for rejecting neoliberal austerity and canceling debt obligations. What this criticism recoiled from admitting was that the capital and import controls would lead to Greece being forced out of the EU as a whole. After thirty-five years of integration, the institutional carapace for capitalism in Greece was provided by the many ways the state apparatus became entangled with the EU. Breaking out of this would have required Syriza as a party and government to be prepared for an immediate systemic rupture. It could certainly be said that Syriza was naive to believe it could stop the European economic torture while remaining in the eurozone, let alone the EU. At the very least, this simultaneously posed two significant questions: Could the Greek state be fundamentally changed while remaining within the EU? And could the EU itself be fundamentally changed from within at the initiative of that state?

For a small country without significant oil resources, a break with the EU would have entailed economic isolation (along the lines of that endured by Cuba after its revolution, yet without the prospect of anything like the geostrategic and economic support Cuba received from the former USSR). The Syriza government faced the intractable contradiction that to fulfill its promise to stop the EU's economic torture, it would have to leave the EU, which would, given the global as well as European balance of forces and the lack of alternative production and consumption capabilities, lead to further economic suffering for an unforeseeable period. Despite the massive popular mobilization the government unleashed by calling the referendum in July to support its position against that of the EU–IMF, the dilemma was the same as it had been when it first entered the state. That the government managed to win reelection in the fall of 2015 while succumbing to and implementing the diktats of the "Institutions" indicated that Kouvelakis's observation when it entered into negotiations back in February still held: "People support the government because the perception they have is that they couldn't act otherwise in that very specific situation. They really see that the balance of forces was extremely uneven."

Costas Douzinas, another prominent London-based Greek intellectual newly elected as a Syriza member of parliament in the fall of 2015, outlined a year later the "three different temporalities" through which the radical left must "simultaneously live" once it enters the state.[5] There is "the time of the present": the dense and difficult time when the Syriza government—"held hostage" to the creditors as a "quasi-protectorate" of the EU and IMF—is required "to implement what they fought against," and thus "to legislate and apply the recessional and socially unjust measures it ideologically rejects." This raises "grave existential issues and problems of conscience" that cannot go away, but can be "soothed through the activation of two other temporalities that exist as traces of futurity in the present time." The second temporality covers "the medium term of three to five years," when time for the government appears "slower and longer" as it probes for the space it needs to implement its "parallel program" so as not only to "mitigate the effects of the memorandum" but also to advance "policies with a clear left direction ... in close contact with the party and the social movements." The third and longest temporality, "the time of the radical left vision," will be reached "only by continuously and simultaneously implementing and undermining the agreement policies." As this third temporality starts unfolding, freed from the neoliberal lambast, "the full programme of the left of the twenty-first century" will emerge."It is a case of escaping into the future, acting now from the perspective of a future perfect, of what will have been. In this sense, the future becomes an active factor of our present."

This scenario was only plausible insofar as what distinguished Syriza from social democratic governments in the neoliberal era, even as it implemented the neoliberal measures forced upon it, was its refusal to embrace neoliberal ideology. The crucial condition for the three temporalities to coexist, however, is precisely the "close contact with the party and the social movements," which Douzinas only mentions in passing. Even in terms of its relations to the party, let alone the social movements, the Syriza government failed to escape from familiar social democratic patterns as it distanced itself from party pressures, and seemed incapable of appreciating the need for activating party cadre to develop social capacities to lay the grounds for temporality two and eventually three. The neglect of the party had already turned to offhand dismissal when the government called the second election of 2015. As so many of its leading cadre left the party in the face of this—including even the general secretary, who also resigned rather than assert the party's independence from the government—the promise that Syriza might escape the fate of social democracy in neoliberal capitalism was left in tatters.[6]

Here is where the lessons to be learned from the Syriza experience become especially important. One of its original leading cadre, Andreas Karitzis, who initially remained in the party while others rushed into the state, has recently articulated these lessons extremely well in arguing that "implementation procedures are the material foundations of a party's political strategy." The advancement of policy goals without consideration of the specific changes that would need to take place in the relevant state apparatuses to actually implement those policies was bound to fail. Decision-making processes at the parliamentary and governmental levels "are just the peak of the iceberg of state policy. Implementing procedures are the mass of the iceberg below the water, i.e., the bulk of state policy . . . . [T]here is no possibility that broad political

decisions can actually shift state policy, whether through in-
advertence or indifference to 'how and who' will implement
these decisions."[7]

The question of "how" was disregarded in the party debates over policy before Syriza's election to government "either because of the inability to offer an answer or because it
was seen as irrelevant in the face of internal party rivalry."
The result of this was that "the dozens of committees that
had been formed reproduced vague political confrontations
instead of outlining specific implementation plans by sector
to overcome obstacles and restructure state functions and institutions with a democratic orientation." Above all,

> at the highest political organs, disagreements over the
> recommended political decision (about the current banks,
> debt, and so on) were tediously repeated as if SYRIZA
> had the ability to implement them . . . . [This] pattern
> of political behaviour that proved particularly problemat-
> ic . . . [as] cadres with a more radical orientation showed
> greater insistence on the lists of demands, which seemed
> to act as a political shield against the focus on "how" and
> thus caused their hesitation to addressing the complexity
> of implementation . . . [while] more moderate cadres usu-
> ally cited the complexities of implementation as the main
> reason for blunting the commitments arising from the
> lists of demands, but without setting the goal of develop-
> ing action plans to overcome such complexities. The end
> result was that the party did not focus on its basic duty:
> developing plans of action to address the difficult "how?"
> of a different policy in the framework of an asphyxiated

political environment. The obsessive adherence to lists of demands that are not attached to plans of action, and the acceptance of difficulties as a reason for adopting a more conventional governance mindset, did not advance the party's operational capability, and did not serve its political strategy.[8]

This strategic failure also proved critically important in relation to the lack of attention (as much or more by those who argued for "Plan B") to drawing on the knowledge and practices of those at the base of the party in closest touch with the social movements so as to enhance the capacities of those who enter the state to try to change it. Strategic planning to this end must, as Karitzis puts it, "not only involve the government, but requires methods of social and political mobilization at multiple levels and of a different nature than movements of social resistance and actions for attaining government power." The potential for a more productive relationship was there, insofar as so many party members at the base were closely involved with the solidarity networks and other community-based initiatives, which initially became

the spark for acknowledging members' skills (formal education, technical expertise, work experience, etc.) and highlighting these abilities and qualifications as important elements for party work as well as facilitating the creative and productive inclusion of people outside its membership. Nonetheless, SYRIZA, as a collective political body, was unable to utilise this enormous skill pool to expand and support its political strategy, because it did not develop the appropriate organisational receptors and "extraction methods" for harnessing human potential.[9]

Perhaps the most unfortunate result was that grassroots participation exhausted itself "in protest or support demonstrations, rather than in substantive and productive engagement," while local and regional party branches "formulated their own activity in the solidarity sector without using the structure, network, infrastructure, and technical expertise of the 'Solidarity for All' initiative or the party's central mechanism."[10] It was ironically those who advanced the ostensibly more radical "Plan B" who seemed to treat state power most instrumentally. Little or no attention was paid by them to how to disentangle a very broad range of state apparatuses from budgetary dependence on EU funding, let alone to the transformations the Greek state apparatuses would have to undergo merely to administer the controls and rationing required to manage the black and gray markets that would have expanded inside and outside the state if Greece exited the eurozone. This was especially problematic given the notorious clientelistic and corrupt state practices that Syriza as a party had been vociferously committed to ending, but once in government did not have the time to change, even where the inclination to do so was still there. When confronted with a question about how to deal with this, one leading advocate of "Plan B" responded privately that in such a moment of rupture it is necessary to shoot people. But this response only raised the bigger question of whom the notoriously

reactionary coercive apparatuses of the Greek state, as un-
changed as they were, would be most likely to listen to, and
most likely to shoot.

Perhaps most tellingly, advocates of "Plan B" showed little
interest in democratizing state apparatuses by linking them
with social movements. This stood in contrast with the minister of social services—herself the key founder of the feder-
ation of solidarity networks, Solidarity4All[11]—who openly
spoke to her frustrations that Syriza MPs, even while paying over a sizeable portion of their salaries to the networks,
insisted that they alone should be the conduits for contact
with solidarity activists in their communities. The minister
of education visited one school a week and did tell teachers,
parents, and students that if they wanted to use the school as
a base for changing social relations in their communities they
would have his support. However, the Ministry of Education
itself did not become actively engaged in promoting the use
of schools as community hubs, neither providing spaces for
activists organizing around food and health services, nor the
appropriate technical education, nor other special programs
to prepare students to spend periods of time in communities,
contributing to adult education and working on community
projects.

Yet it must be said that the social movements themselves
were largely passive and immobilized in this respect, as if
waiting for the government to deliver. Activists from the
networks of food solidarity were rightly frustrated that they
could not get from the minister of agriculture the information

they asked for on the locations of specific crops so they might approach a broader range of farmers. But they did not see it as their responsibility to develop and advance proposals on how the agriculture ministry could have been changed under the Syriza government so as to do this, or more ambitiously so as to identify idle land to be given over to community food production co-ops and to coordinate this across subregions; or even more ambitiously, how the defense ministry might have been changed so that military trucks (at least those sitting idle between demonstrations) could be used to facilitate the distribution of food through the solidarity networks.

The point is this: insofar as the Syriza government has failed the most crucial democratic, let alone revolutionary, test of linking the administration up with popular forces—not just for meeting basic needs but also for planning and implementing the restructuring of economic and social life—there were all too few on the radical left outside the state who saw this strategy as a priority either. The charges of capitulation and betrayal that emanated from an understandably disappointed radical left inside and outside Greece should have been tempered in light of this. There was a marked lack of seriousness, if not dishonesty, behind the tendency to treat the referendum as proving not just the massive public support for resisting further "Troika"-imposed draconian austerity (which was the question actually posed), but also that the same support would have existed for leaving the eurozone, and most likely the EU, in light of the capital and import controls that doing so inevitably would have led to. To say this is not to have any illusions about the EU itself, or about what the Syriza government ended up doing in accommodating to it. Insofar as the majority of Greeks still did want to remain in the EU, Syriza's critics from the left failed to politically acknowledge what the people themselves practically understood, which was precisely the further costs that leaving would have entailed in terms of adding to their suffering, as Greece would have been left economically isolated, or even subject to a military coup or civil war. Syriza did not create the conditions in which people were prepared to risk these consequences. But there is no point in wishing those conditions into existence. The task of democratic socialists is to confront this dilemma.

4

CORBYN'S CHALLENGE: FROM PARTY INSURGENCY TO STATE TRANSFORMATION?

The enormous enthusiasm generated by the campaign to elect Jeremy Corbyn to the leadership of the British Labour Party in the summer of 2015 signaled—amid the delegitimization of neoliberal globalization—the staying power of the shift from protest to politics on the left. This confounded expectations that the disappointment of the high hopes invested in the Syriza government at the beginning of that year would have debilitating effects across the international left. And if it was surprising enough that Corbyn should have been elected as party leader, even more surprising was how clearly his new position initially appeared to be electorally validated when two years later, in June 2017, Corbyn led the Labour party to its largest vote increase in any general election since 1945.

Yet the Corbyn phenomenon once again raised all the old questions associated with the limits and possibilities of democratizing and radicalizing those old working-class parties through which social struggles from below had come to be channeled into the narrow framework of existing capitalist democracies. It is important to recall Ralph Miliband's

sobering judgment in the 1976 *Socialist Register* that "the be-
lief in the effective transformation of the Labour Party into
an instrument of socialist policies is the most crippling of
all illusions to which socialists in Britain have been prone."
Yet it is no less important to recall his observations on the
inability of the socialist left in Britain to create any effective
"organization of its own political formation, able to attract a
substantial measure of support."[1] In the continuing absence
of anything like Syriza's sprouting from the intertwining
roots of Eurocommunism and new social movements in
Greece, it perhaps should not have been quite so surprising
that as the crisis of neoliberalism brought New Labour down
after 2008, the prospect of transforming the Labour Party
would once again emerge as a plausible strategic option for
the British left.

The sudden reinvestment of considerable socialist hope,
energy, and creativity in the Labour Party under Jeremy
Corbyn's leadership was epitomized by the filmmaker Ken
Loach, who in 2013 had stood at the forefront of yet another
futile attempt to launch a serious socialist electoral alternative
(Left Unity).[2] By 2017 Loach could be found making campaign videos for the Labour Party featuring a broad range of
working people demanding "the full fruits of our labour."
To be sure, even under Corbyn, it was still almost unimag-
inable that the Labour Party, absent Greece's legacy of a revolutionary communist political culture, would echo Syriza's
rhetoric in calling for "the creation and expression of the
widest possible, militant, and catalytic political movement

of multidimensional subversion." On the other hand, for all the attempts by New Labour to distance itself from the party's class roots, these remained far more deeply embedded in working-class communities and the trade unions than was the case with Syriza. What fueled popular support for all the recent party insurgencies was a common reaction to neoliberal austerity and the complicity of center-left politicians in it. Yet those who fomented the Corbyn insurgency were far more conscious, based on decades of experience, that making the shift from protest to politics effective would entail a profound transformation in party structures.

The explosion of 1960s activism marked Corbyn's early political development, although the fact that almost the last place most of the activists at that time were initially attracted to was the Labour party already points to one of the most important differences between the earlier attempt to transform the party in the 1970s, spearheaded by Corbyn's mentor Tony Benn, and the one spearheaded by Corbyn himself so many decades later, which became the catalyst for drawing hundreds of thousands of new members to the party. Yet Corbyn's own political formation took place as part of the last serious attempt to effect a radical democratic socialist transformation of the Labour Party amid the terminal crisis of the postwar Keynesian welfare state in the 1970s. Although this crisis had already been defeated by the time Corbyn was first elected as an MP in 1983, he was attracted by Tony Benn's vision to counter the basically undemocratic market alternative to social democracy "now emerging everywhere on the right" by connecting the Labour Party to the political energy fueling the student uprisings, worker militancy, and radical community politics. Benn's message that "our long campaign to democratise power in Britain has, first, to begin in our own movement" above all involved extending "our representative function so as to bring ourselves into a more creative relationship with many organizations that stand outside our membership." The promise of Benn's appeal was thus that "a Labour government will never rule again but will try to create the conditions under which it is able to act as the natural partner of a people, who really mean something more than we thought they did, when they ask for self-government."[3]

The strategic orientation of the Campaign for Labour Party Democracy, or CLPD, to initially concentrate the democratic impulse inward produced intense opposition from the establishment forces in the party, who projected the decade-long intraparty struggle outward as an assault on the integrity of the British state. This blunted the processes of democratic socialist persuasion, education, and mobilization not only so necessary for short-term electoral success but, in a longer-term perspective, for the party to become an active agent of new working-class formation and capacity development. The defeat of democratic forces inside the party, well before the 1983 election, eventually led to the New Labour project of not only accommodating to Thatcherism but also stifling any trace of socialist sentiment as well as intraparty democracy.

As Alex Nunns has shown, the emergence in the early 2000s of a generation of new union leaders began to lay the foundation for a fundamental break with New Labour: "From being the Praetorian guard of the leadership they became the internal opposition . . . [and] embarked on a structural battle with the Blairite machine." This in turn once again highlighted the importance of the old CLPD and its capacity for "navigating the party structures."[4] It also gave new life to the small coterie of MPs in the Socialist Campaign Group of the Parliamentary Labour Party (PLP) (among them, John McDonnell and Diane Abbott stood before Corbyn in the earlier leadership elections, and Jon Trickett had originally been expected to stand in 2015). One of the most important foundations for the Corbyn insurgency was laid almost a decade before when Michael Meacher, a close ally of Benn ever since he was elected as a young MP in 1970, took on as his parliamentary assistant one of the CLPD's original young stalwarts, Jon Lansman, only directing him to stay away from Westminster and instead work full time to revive and deepen the alliance with left-wing constituency and trade-union activists.

It was the ability of the new generation of union leaders to secure their members' votes for Ed Miliband, on the basis of his disavowal of New Labour, which got him elected as leader in 2010. Yet as Richard Seymour observed, "It was an integral part of Ed Miliband's strategy for reviving and rebranding Labour that it should seek a new synthesis of left and right." The alliance he struck with the Blairites who still dominated the PLP countered "pressure from trade unionists and constituency activists to move further to the left than he wished to go."[5] Keeping his distance from Socialist Campaign Group MPs as well as the new union leaders (who his New Labour colleagues still called "the awkward squad"[6]), Miliband initiated a revision of the rules for leadership elections precisely to diminish the influence of the union vote. The new system of one member, one vote, oriented to encouraging a US primary-style vote for leadership candidates nominated from within the PLP, was initially opposed by the left. Yet the unintended consequence of this rule change opened the door for the move from protest to politics in Britain to take the form of almost 200,000 new members and 100,000 more "supporters" signing up to elect Corbyn, beginning the process of making the Labour Party, with over 550,000 members today, the largest in Europe.

Of course, this did not happen spontaneously. It was in good part due to the actual momentum generated by Momentum. The emergence at the time of the Occupy movement of "a cheeky and assertive digital Bennite social media project" called "Red Labour" by an Internet-savvy new generation of activists presaged the creation during the 2015 leadership election campaign, under the leadership of Jon Lansman, of Momentum as a new organization focused on mobilizing new members and supporters behind (and indeed in front of) Corbyn. With a database that became its primary asset, Momentum activists not only played a crucial role in getting Corbyn elected as leader, but also reelected again a year later in the face of the revolt supported by most of the Labour MPs. Even while soon surpassing the CLPD's earlier successes in mobilizing the majority of constituency delegates to vote for the left's resolutions at the annual party conference, the energy and creativity of Momentum's young activists was especially evident in organizing "The World Transformed" as a parallel event of radical art and discussion that sharply contrasted with the trade show atmosphere under New Labour.

Perhaps the most significant aspect of the June 2017 election, very much more due to Momentum's strategic electoral activity both on the ground in canvassing as well as through the Internet, was the greatly increased turnout by young people to vote Labour. This was achieved despite almost two years of constant denigration of Corbyn by many of his own MPs being amplified across the whole spectrum of the mainstream media, as well as against the drag of a central party machine more concerned with vetting than welcoming new members. With the greatest electoral support coming not only from students but also from working-class voters under thirty-five, especially from the semiskilled, unskilled, and unemployed workers among them, the Labour electorate suddenly had a remarkably young cast, with a potentially very important shift in the party's class base. The last time anything like this happened was a half century before, in the two elections of the mid-1960s, when a new generation of working-class voters belied the widespread notion that class political differentiation was a thing of the past by voting Labour in such large numbers. It was only after the profoundly disappointing experience of a Labour government desperately attempting to manage the growing contradictions of the British "mixed economy" and its "special relationship" with the American empire that a great many of the young working-class voters turned away from the Labour Party by the time of the 1970 election.

Labour's remarkable electoral success in 2017, especially among young working-class people, was based on the common revulsion against austerity among both private- and public-sector workers. This stands in sharp contrast to the former's impatience with, if not hostility toward, the latter's strikes against the austerity policies of the Labour government during the "winter of discontent" just before the election of Thatcher. The much more sympathetic attitude to the plight of public employees forty years later was powerfully captured by the positive reception to Momentum's satirical campaign video (visited by no less than a third of all Facebook users in Britain), which—after featuring a home-care worker, a firefighter, and a policeman on the job turning to the camera to say "I am paid too much"—ends with a man in a pinstriped suit and bowler hat turning to the camera just before entering his London mansion to say "I am not paid enough."

Yet Corbyn's team "seemed unsure of what to do with its new recruits" beyond the "highly impressive get-out-the-vote operation," as Tom Blackburn, a leading Momentum activist in the classically industrial city of Salford, pointed out in an especially insightful article in *New Socialist* immediately after the election. Noting that "the Corbynite base as a whole remains somewhat inexperienced"—especially in terms of its ability "to actively cultivate popular support for a radical political alternative, rather than assuming that there is sufficient support already latent, just waiting to be tapped into"—Blackburn argued that "the leadership must now start to provide its rank-and-file supporters with clear guidance and encouragement if this project is to progress further." What this especially required was "clarity and honesty about the scale of the task facing Labour's new left, and the nature of that task as well—to reestablish the Labour Party as a campaigning force in working-class communities, to democratise its policymaking structures, and to bring through the next generation of Labour left cadres, candidates, and activists." In this respect, the priority now needed to become transforming Labour, especially since "an unsupportive bureaucracy could simply withhold the resources and logistical support necessary to make radical community organising a reality nationwide. Members looking to open up local parties and experiment with new methods of organising can currently expect little support from an unreformed Labour HQ." None of this was to suggest that

> the rank-and-file Labour left should just sit around and wait for help from on high before organising in their communities. Indeed, there is already a great deal of highly useful and relevant experience of grassroots organising among Labour members—the hands-on experience of anti-cuts campaigners and trade union activists

is already substantial. Rank-and-file initiative can make substantial achievements. But for this sort of approach to solidly take hold nationwide, an attentive and supportive central party apparatus will be invaluable.[7]

The election of Momentum candidates as constituency and youth representatives to the party's National Executive Committee, and the NEC's appointment of one of the new generation of left trade union staff as the new general secretary, appeared to augur well for this (although the manner of the latter's selection by prior agreement between the party and union leader's offices did not). The establishment at party headquarters of a new "community organising unit" to work with constituency Labour parties and trade unions to build alliances and campaign on key local issues was also a promising development. For its part, Momentum's tactical caution to avoid being drawn into a media-fueled hysteria over the "reselection" of all sitting MPs, as had been the case with CLPD's reform effort in the 1970s, did not divert it from winning support among party branches and conference delegates for concrete proposals for "a democratic selection process for the twenty-first century," nor from getting many Momentum-backed candidates nominated at the parliamentary as well as the municipal council level.

Especially in relation to the intraparty Democracy Review[8] that was set up by NEC, the kinds of fundamental changes Max Shanly called for in the youth wing of the party were especially important: "The role of political education is to end one's alienation from ideas—and alongside recruitment and retention, our task must be to build the political and organisational quality of our party's youth in order to both understand and resist capitalism." Yet in the party as a whole "political education—the very bread and butter of the socialist movement—has been put on the backburner; when our members are taught, they are taught to follow, not to lead." Changing this antiquated system would have to go right down to the level of constituency parties in order to remold them into "hubs of ongoing discussion, education, and culture."[9]

This needed to be taken much further. To credibly stress the possibilities rather than the limits of changing the Labour Party required posing a fundamental challenge to the way the party has traditionally been rooted in the working class via the trade unions. Indeed, what needed to be remembered in this new conjuncture is that the defeat of the last socialist attempt to transform the Labour Party, in which young people like Jeremy Corbyn and Jon Lansman first cut their teeth, was that it was the left-wing union leadership who, having supported it through their block vote at a party conference, pulled the plug in the face of the inevitable divisions it created inside the labor movement.[10] The traditional relationship between the unions and the party reproduced a division of labor that proved incapable of nourishing and renewing working-class formation and the development of democratic capacities. In this context, the support Corbyn secured from much of the union leadership very much needed to be turned into a challenge to the left-wing union leaders to validate their role in the current attempt to change the Labour Party by changing their own organizations, not least through explicit socialist cadre development among their memberships.

In the face of the Labour Party's traditional power structures and parliamentarist orientations, let alone the powerful forces that still sustain New Labour's expression of contemporary capitalist dynamics, the struggle inside the party was always bound to be long and bitter, and its outcome very uncertain, even after important victories for the left in intraparty procedures and leadership selection. Indeed, it is to be expected that those determined to resist and reverse these gains, and more broadly to undermine socialist currents at the level of the leadership and the base, will always be prepared to ramp up their efforts and push them outward as each new set of elections approaches in the hope that this will increase their leverage in the intraparty battle. Appreciating this challenge is critical, and learning how to counter it effectively is one of the key reasons that political education at the base of the party, as well as in the unions and the social movements, is, however daunting and difficult, so crucial.

CHALLENGING THE BRITISH STATE?

Before 2015 it would have seemed most unlikely that among those looking for the renewal of socialist possibilities in the twenty-first century, it would be developments in the British Labour Party that would attract the most international attention. That this became the case after 2015 was a credit to the enthusiasm and creativity of a new generation of socialist activists in Britain and the political perseverance and dedication of a coterie of long-committed socialists associated with Jeremy Corbyn. Yet if the promise of the election of a Corbyn government in Britain was not to lead to heady euphoria quickly followed by profound disappointment on the left internationally, as was the case with Syriza in Greece, British realities needed to be kept in sober perspective.

It is important to appreciate the very limited extent to which socialist commitment has, so far, taken shape as socialist strategy inside the Labour Party. At best it might be said that socialists in the leadership and at the base may be seen as engaged in trying to shift the balance of forces inside the party, and outside it in relation to the unions and social movements—and indeed, even in Momentum—so as to bring the party to the point that a serious socialist strategy might be developed.

Labour's popular 2017 election manifesto, with its radical articulation of an economic program "for the many not the few," represented a conspicuous turn away from neoliberal austerity and the accommodation of New Labour governments to the Thatcherite legacy.[11] This was to be accomplished through progressive taxation measures, the enhancement of a broad array of public services as well as union and workers' rights, and the renationalization of railways and public utilities. It set out an industrial strategy to create an "economy that works for all" through the strategic use of public procurement and national and regional investment banks. Although much of this was cast as a "new deal for business," oriented toward making British industry more regionally balanced and internationally competitive, underpinned by what it calls a "successful international financial industry," the emphasis clearly fell on state actions and legal changes that would require finance and industry to make their activities more "diverse" and "socially useful" to meet the needs of workers, consumers, and communities.

More telling regarding the socialist orientation of Corbyn's inner circle may be the "Alternative Models of Ownership" report, commissioned by John McDonnell and released a few days before the election.[12] Though not official party policy, the report stressed the role of municipal public ownership and procurement policies to seed and nurture worker and community cooperatives in order to encourage broad discussion of new socialist strategies. The "Alternative Models" report especially revived the concern, voiced by the Labour left ever since the nationalizations of the 1945 Labour government, to avoid top-down corporate management in publicly owned enterprises by encouraging new forms of industrial democracy as well as accountability to "diverse publics." And it also reflected the thinking of the Labour "new left" about new forms of public ownership that could draw directly on the expertise and insights of workers on the shop floor, along the lines pioneered by the Lucas Aerospace shop stewards in the 1970s and the Greater London Council in the 1980s.

This orientation exactly characterized McDonnell's own strategic perspective, which was explicitly to "not try to recreate the nationalised industries of the past . . . whose management was often too distant, too bureaucratic, and too removed from the reality of those at the forefront of delivering services." Instead, the nationalizations of essential industries by a Labour government now would be treated as "an opportunity for us to put those industries in the hands of those who run and use them."[13] This was part and parcel of seeing, as McDonnell put it in his speech to the September 2018 Labour Party conference, democracy as "at the heart of our socialism—and extending it should always be our goal . . . at the heart of our programme is the greatest extension of economic democratic rights that this country has ever seen. It starts in the workplace."[14]

This would be enacted through legislation mandating that each year, 1 percent of the shares of all large corporations (covering some 40 percent of the private-sector workforce) be transferred into an Inclusive Ownership Fund (IOF), maxing out at a total of 10 percent ownership accumulated over ten years. Workers' representatives would have unspecified voting rights in their company of employment based on the shares allocated, but they could not trade those shares. This fund would pay out dividends to individual workers in each firm of up to a maximum of £500 a year each. After the distribution of the dividends to workers, the balance of the funds—an estimated £2.1 billion by the fifth year of the program, totaling one-third of 1 percent of the British state's central annual expenditures—would be treated as a social dividend that "could be spent supporting our public services and social security." This itself is not substantially different from a modest corporate tax.[15] The cap on dividend payments to employees (under 2 percent of the average annual income of British workers), as well as the rough equalization of dividend payments across firms and the contributions to universal programs, were intended to prevent the emergence of excessive inequality between workers in different sectors.

This plan clearly fell well short of representing a strategy for achieving a transition from capitalism to socialism, whether as conceived in the old Clause IV commitment to "the common ownership of the means of production, distribution, and exchange and the best obtainable system of popular administration and control of each industry or service"; or, as it was later more vaguely put on the Labour left, as taking over "the commanding heights of the economy." No less important, such proposals for the expansion of co-ops and workers' control at the enterprise level, while legitimately raising the *potential* transformative contribution of workers' collective knowledge, underplay how far workers' *actual* capacities have been constricted under capitalism. Moreover, the emphasis on decentralized forms of common ownership usually skirts the crucial question of how to integrate and coordinate enterprises, sectors, and regions through democratic economic planning processes, which are so necessary to avoid reproducing the types of particularistic and dysfunctional competitive market behaviour that socialists want to transcend.[16]

What was perhaps most problematic was the glaring silence on how the promotion of a high-tech, internationally competitive industrial strategy relates to the development of a strategy of transformation to socialism.[17] And related to this, there were real strategic costs associated with the understandable reluctance to publicly broach the vexing question of how and when to introduce capital controls, so essential to investment planning as well as to countering the blackmail of governments via capital flight in open financial markets. In contrast with the New Left insurgency of the 1970s, there is a marked avoidance today of openly discussing the question of the need to turn the whole financial system into a public utility. In the absence of this, effective socialist economic and social restructuring of Britain, let alone decentralization of significant democratic decisions to the local community level, cannot be realized.

This is not to say that merely calling for sweeping immediate nationalizations really addresses these strategic problems. As Tony Benn told the 1979 Labour Party conference in speaking for the NEC against adopting Militant's "resolutionary" posture of demanding the immediate nationalization of the top two hundred industrial and financial corporations, this simply failed to take seriously what it meant to be "a party of democratic, socialist reform." While averring he was a "Clause IV socialist, becoming more so as the years go by," Benn nevertheless rightly insisted that any serious socialist strategy had to begin from "the usual problems of the reformer: we have to run the economic system to protect our people who are locked into it while we change the system."[18]

This stark dilemma was also seriously addressed by Seumas Milne (the former *Guardian* journalist who became Corbyn's right-hand man) in his 1989 coauthored book, *Beyond the Casino Economy*. On the one hand, the book argued that "one of the necessary conditions for a socialist society would be to turn [the top] few hundred corporations into democratically owned and accountable public bodies." On the other, it conceded that "in the foreseeable circumstances of the next few years, the socialization of all large-scale private enterprise seems highly unlikely," which limited "what can plausibly be proposed as part of a feasible programme for a Labour government in the coming years—even one elected in an atmosphere of radical expectations."[19]

The crucial point here is not to stubbornly insist on an immediate radicalization of policy that can only represent ineffective sloganeering. The same longstanding constraints of the internal balance of forces in the party, as well as electoral ones, shaped the 2017 Labour manifesto. The measure of the Corbyn leadership in this regard should not have been how explicitly socialist its policies were, but rather the extent to which it problematized how to implement reform measures in such ways as to advance, rather than close off, future socialist possibilities. That is, to enhance—through the development of class, party, and state capacities—the possibility of realizing socialist goals.

It might especially have been hoped that Labour's "Digital Democracy Manifesto" would have pointed in that direction. Unfortunately, it betrayed "a rather narrow image of technology that concentrates on the Internet, end-users, and 'networked individuals' ... an image of publicness in the form of networks that nevertheless has security and privacy at its heart," as Nina Power has noted. The result is that the report contributes very little to how "the new digital technologies help us to think about democratic economic planning," as Power herself went on to do for the care services sector of the economy.[20] Power's recommendation needs to be extended to thinking through the role of digital technology in the economic planning needed to turn the "Alternative Models of Ownership" report into a socialist strategy. Still more ambitiously, it should be applied to thinking through how to develop the planning capacities to transform financial services, Britain's dominant economic sector, into a public utility.

Unlike the early 1970s, when Tony Benn and his new left allies controlled the National Executive's policy committees and were able to formulate a reasonably coherent and comprehensive industrial strategy (which was almost entirely ignored once Labour was reelected in 1974), Corbyn and his team inherited nothing of that nature. Experts in a wide variety of fields have many creative ideas for progressive policies that a Labour government could use, including on macroeconomic policy, banking, taxation, pensions, debt, and ways of restoring the primacy of the public interest in the funding and management of the public infrastructure. The party machine has, however, hardly tapped into them. The 2017 manifesto, hastily drafted when the snap election was called, largely drew on policy proposals the unions had put forward in previous

years and had plenty of omissions and weaknesses, some due
to the speed with which it had to be composed. Whole areas
of policy clearly needed far more radical measures and, as one
astute critic of the manifesto put it, "a radical reorientation of
economic priorities away from the industrial capitalist obsession with economic growth" if ecological catastrophe was to
be avoided.[21] Another crucial element missing from the manifesto was any significant move toward democratizing the state.

After the 2017 election, it fell to McDonnell and Rebecca
Long-Bailey in particular, as the shadow ministers responsible for finance and industry respectively, to flesh out Labour's
industrial, investment, and environmental plans.[22] In March
2018, McDonnell affirmed (notably in a *Financial Times* interview) that "our objectives are socialist . . . [which] means
an irreversible shift in the balance of power and wealth in
favour of working people . . . . When we go into government, everyone will be in government."[23] Important in this
regard was his determination, conveyed in his 2018 speeches
at the Labour Party conference and Momentum's The World
Transformed event, to "reprogram the Treasury, rewriting its
rule books on how it makes decisions about what, when, and
where to invest" so as to finally bring to an end its being used
"as a barrier against putting power back into the hands of
the people." This expressly included setting up a "Public and
Community Ownership Unit" in the Treasury that would
"bring in the external expertise we will need."

More detailed plans for structural changes at the Bank of England were outlined in an independent report, commissioned

by McDonnell, that proposed "restructuring and relocating core Bank of England functions [to] provide a counterweight to the dominance of London."[24] This would not only involve establishing regional offices "to ensure that productive lending is geared toward local businesses," but moving some of the main Bank of England offices, even including the Monetary Policy Committee, to Birmingham. There it would sit alongside the offices of a new National Investment Bank and a Strategic Investment Board, which would be responsible for generating and allocating investment under Labour's industrial strategy, along with a National Transformation Fund, responsible for Labour's infrastructure program. This geographic shift was seen as essential for realizing the report's main policy proposals: beyond setting a 3 percent productivity growth target, these included establishing credit guidelines to shift private bank lending away from real estate, discretionary corporate bond purchasing to stimulate investment and reduce the cost of the infrastructure program, and aiding the National Investment Board by using the still mainly publicly owned Royal Bank of Scotland as its banking arm.

In itself, this plan was still far from anything that might be called a socialist strategy for structural change. Not because of the report's sensible insistence that decision making must reflect the views of "scientists, researchers, engineers, and technology experts," nor merely because it said that "private sector investment is critical" and that all the institutions involved "must encourage an entrepreneurial spirit." More significantly, the national models it offered for a Labour government's industrial strategy to emulate went so far beyond social democratic Norway or even Germany as to actually include such uncompromisingly capitalist regimes as Singapore, South Korea, Japan—and, most notably, even the US itself. Lurking here was perhaps the most problematic aspect of Labour's industrial strategy: its silence on the question of how the promotion of internationally competitive export enterprises, within the framework of global capitalism, relates to the development of a transformational socialist strategy.[25]

Notably, McDonnell signaled to Momentum's participants at The World Transformed in 2017 that plans were in hand to deal with capital flight or a run on the pound.[26] His public silence since then on the difficult question of how and when to introduce controls over the movement of capital was entirely understandable, given the subject's political sensitivity and the importance of the financial sector's foreign exchange earnings. But policies on this issue were no less necessary than industrial policies if a socialist-led government was to be able to direct investment where it was needed and prevent capital flight. The logical response to a refusal by companies to invest for long-term productivity growth would be to introduce capital controls and investment planning. But this could not be done without developing the state's capacity to transform financial services, Britain's dominant economic sector, into a public utility—even taking advantage of the possibility of starting with the Royal Bank of Scotland, still largely in public ownership after having been rescued in the wake of the 2007–2008 crisis.[27]

It makes sense to concentrate on expanding social ownership where openings exist, such as in radically democratizing
the provision of social services and, as Corbyn and McDonnell emphasized, in running the renationalized companies
in exemplary democratic ways that balance worker participation, community interests, and the larger national interest. This step holds the promise of inspiring and mobilizing
workers behind the expansion of public investments, especially those needed to implement a "Green New Deal" defined in terms of "a public-led society-wide mission shaped
by workers, unions, and communities ... through a transformational change in the forms and directions of investment,
ownership, planning, and control in society."[28] Moreover, the
Monbiot Report's proposals for the gradual but potentially
large-scale transfer of land into various forms of common
ownership—explicitly presented as the type of "non-reformist reform" first advanced in the UK by André Gorz's 1968
Socialist Register essay—could have more transformative implications than did the 1945 Labour government's adoption
of the Beveridge Report's welfare measures.[29]

Various proposals advanced by policy circles supportive of
McDonnell have also addressed how to deploy the substantive procurement weight of the goods and services provided
or at least paid for by state and para-state institutions (e.g.,
health, education, social care, public transportation, water,
electricity). And this has been persuasively connected to the
need to impose planning agreements on companies anxious
to get public contracts in the "foundational" sector of the

economy.[30] Such planning agreements could indeed represent a meaningful step toward the socialization of these companies and more substantive democratization, while working to establish exemplary standards of transparency, product quality, and working conditions that could influence expectations in other workplaces. Similarly, there is an opportunity in state and para-state social services and programs—a very significant part of the economy—to not only deliver needed programs, but also to show that reforms inspired from a socialist perspective could involve participatory planning structures at the local level. The goal would be to make such programs more democratic and constructive of organic social relationships among unions, users, and communities.[31]

All these considerations were dwarfed, of course, by the devastating defeat Corbyn suffered at the hand of Boris Johnson in December 2019. Amidst the ongoing paralysis of Parliament over Brexit, as Corbyn became ever more trapped in what is known in the UK as 'the Westminster bubble', and his team tried to make him appear more like a normal politician, he looked less and less comfortable. On top of this his determination 'to go high when they went low' appeared to suggest passivity in the face of the disingenuous and absurd charges that he supported IRA terrorists and was an anti-Semite. Corbyn could not and would not disown his anti-imperialist record, but failing to respond to gross distortions of it cost Labour dearly in the 2019 election. And although the 2019 manifesto was actually more coherent and progressive, especially in making the environmental crisis, rather than the need for export competitiveness, the over-arching framework for the radical industrial strategy, now called the Green Industrial Revolution, it did not have the kind of impact on the election that the 2017 manifesto had.

The 2019 election also revealed the relative weakness of Momentum activists in the post-industrial regions where the need for engagement in class struggles, organizing and education was most acute. Indeed, Labour's defeat in 2019 underlined the limits of what could be done without fundamental changes in the party itself, very little of which had been accomplished during the Corbyn years, especially in terms of engaging directly in struggles and activities at the level of the community as well as the workplace, and fostering the social as well as political networks to create links across diverse working class communities and workplaces. Most of the vast increase in membership during the Corbyn years occurred through affiliations at the national level rather than through a local constituency party. And very few of them, including Momentum activists, attended regular local party meetings. What this meant was that even if Corbyn had won the 2019 election, the manifold obstacles to accomplishing much, inside or outside the EU, would have included not only opposition from among his own MPs but also from the insufficient support that had been generated even at the base of the party for transforming the state.

5

SANDERS'S CHALLENGE:
ECONOMIC DEMOCRACY BEYOND
"RESPONSIBLE CAPITALISM"?

"Election days come and go. But political and social rev-
olutions that attempt to transform our society never end."
The speech with which Bernie Sanders closed his Democratic primary election campaign in 2016 began with these
sentences; it ended by expressing the hope that future his-
torians would trace all the way back to the "political revolution" of 2016 "how our country moved forward into
reversing the drift toward oligarchy, and created a government which represents all the people and not just the few."[1]
It is tempting to treat as ersatz the rhetoric of revolution
deployed here, taking the meaning of the word from the
sublime to the ridiculous, or from tragedy to farce. The last
time an American politician vying for the presidency issued
a call for a political revolution it came from Ronald Rea-
gan. But for all the limits of Sanders's populist campaign,
the national attention and massive support garnered by a
self-styled democratic socialist who positively associated the
term revolution with the struggle against class inequality in
fact represented a major discursive departure in American

political life, which can be a resource for further socialist organizing.

Of course, the specific policy measures advanced by Sanders were, as he constantly insisted, reforms that had at some point been introduced in other capitalist societies. But when the call for public Medicare for all, or free college tuition, or infrastructure renewal through direct public employment, is explicitly attached to a critique of a ruling class that wields corporate and financial power through the direct control of parties, elections, and the media, it goes beyond the bounds of what can properly be dismissed as mere reformism, even if the demands hardly evoke what the call for bread, land, and peace did in 1917. And it is no less a significant departure, especially in the US, to make class inequality the central theme of a political campaign in a manner designed to span and penetrate race and gender divisions to the end of building a more coherent class force. By explicitly posing the question of who stands to benefit more from high-quality public health care and education and well-compensated work opportunities than African Americans and Latinos, Sanders highlighted the need to move beyond the ghettos of identity.

The key question was whether Sanders's campaign could lay the groundwork for an ongoing political movement capable of effecting this "political revolution." Sanders's argument during the campaign that he could be sustained in the White House amid a hostile Congress and imperial state apparatus by a "mass movement" marching on Washington, DC was not very convincing. Much more serious was his call after he lost the primary campaign for a shift from protest to politics at every level, including "school boards, city councils, county commissions, state legislatures, and governorships."

The very fact that the Sanders campaign was class-focused rather than class-rooted may have been an advantage here. It opened space for a new politics that could try to become more "rooted" in the sense of being grounded in working-class struggles but committed to the radical transformation of the generally exhausted institutions of the labor movement. This transformation ranges across turning union branches into centers of working-class life, leading the fight for collective public services, breaking down the oligarchic relationship between leaders and led, contributing to building the broadest member capacities, emphasizing the importance of expressing a clearer class sensibility, and even becoming ambitious enough to introduce socialist ideas. This also applies to workers action centers, which have spread across the US but are so often overwhelmed by having to reproduce themselves financially in order to continue providing vital services to Black, Latino, immigrant, and women workers. Becoming more class-rooted and effective would require building the institutional capacities to creatively organize workers in different sectors into new city-wide organizations, as well as develop a coordinating national infrastructure.

A new class politics cannot emerge ex nihilo, however. The 2016 Sanders campaign, initiated by an outsider in the Democratic Party, confirmed that if you are not heard in the media you are not broadly heard. Yet whatever the advantages of initially mobilizing from within established institutions in this respect, the impossibility of a political revolution taking place under the auspices of the Democratic Party needs to be directly faced. After it had become clear he would not clinch the nomination, Sanders and the movement that had begun to take shape around him appeared at risk of falling into a myopic strategy of internally transforming and democratizing the Democratic Party. In part, this is one of the contradictions in Sanders's choice to run as a Democrat. While the 2016 Sanders campaign showed that Democratic Party institutions offer certain bases from which to advance a left politics—lending his campaign a certain legitimacy and credibility within mainstream discourse—in the long run, an alternative political pole will have to be constructed around which social struggles can condense.

It was far from surprising that the thousands of Sanders supporters who gathered at the People's Summit in Chicago after the primary campaign ended did not come there to found a new party. What happened there, as Dan La Botz described it, "was about vision, not organization or strategy," so that one could at best only hear "the sound made by the zeitgeist passing though the meeting rooms and the halls, brushing up against us, making its way, sometimes gracefully, sometimes clumsily, to the future."[2] One key test had to be whether, as "the zeitgeist" made its way, lessons would be learned from the US Labor Party project of the 1990s, and whether, while escaping the traces of either Bolshevik sectarianism or "third-world" romanticism, the forces behind Sanders would also abandon the naive admiration for Canadian and European social democracy that has long characterized so much of the US left, and especially the tiny Democratic Socialists of America within the Democratic Party itself.[3]

The remarkable growth of the Democratic Socialists of America after the 2016 Sanders campaign, taking its membership from a few thousand of mostly ancient vintage to some sixty thousand mostly youthful activists, has completely altered the profile of the American left. To a significant extent, Sanders has led the way in creating an opening for the new socialist discourse, as well as in working through his presidential campaign to not just win the election, but also to build a lasting working-class movement. In his 2020 bid for the Democratic nomination, Sanders has built on the achievements of his 2016 campaign in this regard by supporting strikes and other working-class struggles—even using his campaign organization to encourage supporters to march on picket lines in their area, and to alert immigrant rights activists about impending ICE raids. Sanders's efforts to increase the confidence, capacities, and expectations of the working class have contributed substantially to the emergence of a new socialist movement in the US. DSA members have especially taken advantage of the opening this has created to rebuild the labor movement, with particularly strong success in an impressive series of teachers' strikes across the country, from West Virginia to California.[4]

In addition to the concern to break with austerity and implement radical reforms to the immediate benefit of working people, the new socialist discourse Sanders and the DSA fostered has focused considerably on the crucial issue of economic democratization. This has created important political space for casting a new challenge to capitalist control over investment, production, and distribution in a positive light. Yet what has been proposed is exceedingly modest, primarily involving various schemes for partial worker ownership and participation in management at the level of the firm. This obviously reflects the current balance of class forces as well as a lack of the strategic clarity and political capacities left forces can bring to bear today.

RESPONSIBLE CAPITALISM OR DEMOCRATIC SOCIALISM?

The need for strategic clarity was visible in Sanders's 2016 call to fundamentally change the "rigged economy" by "breaking up the banks" rather than turn them into public utilities.[5] Though this was less a focus of his 2020 campaign, Sanders continued to push such legislation in Congress. At the same time, Sanders's call for workers to be granted seats on corporate boards of directors, and support for new forms of worker ownership, stimulated much discussion among the socialist left around the question of democratizing the economy. Sanders boldly presented these policies as part of a fundamental economic transformation—a challenge to capital and a step toward building a socialist society. Yet they also join a range of proposals that are explicitly—sometimes emphatically—*not* socialist, including a somewhat similar plan by Elizabeth Warren to grant workers seats on corporate boards, limit executives' ability to exercise stock options, and promote "corporate social responsibility." Warren's proposed "Accountable Capitalism Act" is explicitly aimed at rejuvenating capitalism by making corporations more "inclusive" and "accountable," while reining in the outsize power of finance.[6] Even aside from her proud declaration that "I am a capitalist to my bones," the fact that her plan is modeled on German "codetermination" should serve as a warning as to its limits, given how this framework has been used in Germany in recent decades to impose relentless wage restraint and competitive restructuring.

Warren's reform proposals have generally been the most detailed of any advanced among progressive liberal and moderate social democratic politicians today. Her central argument is that, in the neoliberal era, "the obsession with maximizing shareholder returns effectively means America's biggest companies have dedicated themselves to making the rich even richer." This "obsession," she argues, has been primarily responsible for the increasing social inequality, declining wages, and economic stagnation that have characterized the neoliberal period. Warren claims financial pressure, combined with their own stock holdings, has led managers to "short-termist" investment strategies, effectively looting their companies by diverting capital from useful investment to "buying back" shares of their company's stock to manipulate the share price. As a result, "good jobs" are disappearing and corporate investment has become a simple matter of handing money out to the super rich. Moreover, this underinvestment means companies are "setting themselves up to fail." To remedy this, Warren proposes preventing managers and directors from selling shares within five years of receiving them, or within three years of executing a buyback. She also suggests issuing federal corporate charters requiring firms to act as "benefit corporations," serving a range of stakeholders—including workers, consumers, and communities—rather than just shareholders. This would be supported by granting employees the right to elect 40 percent of corporate boards of directors, which will "give workers a stronger voice in corporate decision making at large companies." By increasing the autonomy of managers from investor discipline, corporations will supposedly engage in the kind of investment that generated the "good jobs" and rising standards of living that characterized the postwar managerial period.[7]

Warren's proposal is based on the "stakeholder capitalism" model, which assumes that the corporation can balance different interests that are not necessarily in conflict. Yet corporations are not impartial arbiters among different "stakeholders," but crystallizations of capitalist power. Nor is this power merely *economic*, it is also *political*. Corporations pursue state regulatory and tax structures that are conducive to their continued accumulation and competitiveness—policies that worker-appointed directors would be very susceptible to endorsing, even if they came at the expense of other workers or the environment. Should a firm fail to perform the capitalist function, it will suffer higher costs and reduced returns relative to its competitors—and therefore find less capital available for investment and expansion, leading to cutbacks, layoffs, and possibly bankruptcy. Clearly, no directors, no matter who elected them, would favor a strategy inclined to end this way. Rather than profits always appearing as "too much" (since they are the most obvious sign of exploitation, they can be the most direct source of class-consciousness), they must be defended, even increased if possible. While worker representatives on boards, as in Germany, have tried to resist profit-driven restructuring at the expense of jobs, these defenses have not been able to overcome the relentless pressures of competitiveness.

Warren's concern to fix what existing manufacturing firms do or don't do requires a much more radical restructuring of the economy, especially the financial sector, which even nonfinancial sectors would themselves aggressively resist because of the functionality of finance to their domestic and global activities. Managers of nonfinancial corporations have relied on international finance to integrate the global economy while managing fluctuating exchange rates and other risks associated with world trade through derivatives trading and other forms of financialization. Nonfinancial corporations also depend on finance to execute mergers and acquisitions, and consumer credit markets to maintain consumption to compensate for stagnant wages. These central features of neoliberalism are untouched by Warren's proposals.[8]

Warren's plan aims to reinforce, not challenge, the power of large manufacturing corporations. Throughout the neoliberal period, managers of nonfinancial corporations have launched numerous failed efforts to defend themselves against financial discipline by setting up anti-takeover defenses in the form of golden parachutes, poison pills, and state regulations. Were Warren's bill implemented, it might succeed in granting industrial managers the protection from financial investors they have long sought. It has been well documented that workers generally side with management in conflicts with outsiders; however, the tension between industrial managers and outside investors for corporate control does not negate their unity in seeking to restrain effective worker (or democratic) control over the corporation.[9]

Contrary to the supposed corrupting influence of financial "short-termism," the rising living standards of postwar capitalism rested on more than merely a specific model of corporate governance. It also depended on relatively high union density. Though of course highly limited and dependent on capital for jobs, trade unions nonetheless constitute an institutional mechanism for reproducing forms of worker solidarity and agency that, in crucial respects, contradicts the logic of capital, articulating social needs that capital tends to ignore—including those necessary for its own reproduction, such as a healthy, properly fed and housed workforce. Without organized workers' struggles against capitalist exploitation, competitive pressure to allocate capital as efficiently as possible—within firms as well as across the economy as a whole—means that downward pressure on wages would continue to produce economic inequality and precarity. A strong trade union movement in many ways represents a more substantial form of economic democracy than granting workers seats on boards, or for that matter extending their ownership stakes in individual firms. While this still begs the question of how to "take capital away from capital," Warren's plan integrates workers with corporate power in a way that could reinforce the very financialized neoliberalism she seeks to challenge, by undermining the class independence necessary to confront it.

While proposing that workers be allocated 40 percent of the seats on corporate boards, Warren's plan does not entail transferring stock ownership to them. Sanders goes further than Warren not just in calling for workers to have 45 percent of the seats on boards, but also in placing great emphasis on giving workers stock ownership as well. Although promising these reforms would herald a historic shift in class power, Sanders's plan actually risks, like Warren's plan, deepening the embeddedness of workers within "their" corporations. Giving workers an ownership stake in corporate competitiveness is unlikely to contribute to building the kind of counterpower to capitalist logic that is necessary to bring about a genuinely democratic economy.

Sanders has long been a supporter of extending employee stock ownership plans (ESOPs), at least since the 1980s when he was the mayor of Burlington, Vermont. More recently, Sanders has played a key role in supporting the Vermont Employee Ownership Center, established in 2001 and a model for legislation he has introduced in Congress.[10] With Sanders's decades-long support, Vermont today has the largest per capita number of employee-owned firms of any state in the US. As he put it in a 2018 speech: "What ESOPs are about . . . is saying, for a start, that you can have a more productive and profitable company when you listen to all of the people who are working . . . productivity goes up, profits go up, morale goes up. People do not bemoan the fact they have to go to work; they feel proud of the company they are going to work for, and they want to do everything possible to make that company better."[11] This articulation points to the limits of ESOPs insofar as they may tend to promote *even deeper* alliances between workers, managers, and owners than is the case with merely granting workers seats on boards.

Sanders's plan for worker ownership is similar to what has been proposed by Corbyn and McDonnell in the UK.[12] One of the most striking features of discussion about these plans has been the assumption that by owning shares, workers will not only benefit from dividend payments, but also gain *control* over corporate strategy. Even if these reforms are a radical departure from the neoliberal fixation on shareholder value, they are clearly limited and would fall far short of the socialization of capital and economic democratization; their basic thrust appears to be about *distribution* not *democratization*. Worker share ownership does not amount to greater control unless workers are ready to demand it and have the capacity to carry out that demand. There is a tendency to underestimate the complexities of internal corporate decision-making, which extends beyond the level of boards to include various layers of formal and informal decision-making and access to internal and external information. For workers to exert influence within a corporation would therefore demand levels of confidence and capacities explicitly suppressed under capitalism, along with access to knowledge and links to sympathetic specialists ("red experts") that cannot be assumed but need to be systematically developed. Even then, such "control" would be highly limited and constrained by the logic of private accumulation unless connected to a broader strategy for socializing the economy. Introducing a new dimension of working-class fragmentation, as these plans risk doing, could make this more, not less, difficult. Despite the radical political vision McDonnell has articulated, even his emphasis on decentralized forms of common ownership skirts the crucial question of how to integrate and coordinate enterprises, sectors, and regions through democratic economic planning processes.

Nevertheless, because they involve transferring shares, comparisons have been drawn between Sanders's and McDonnell's plans and the "Meidner Plan" of the 1970s. This plan emerged from a Swedish labor movement that still had the capacity to advance radical changes even as the social democratic era was drawing to a close and the balance of class forces had already begun to shift toward capital. The Meidner Plan involved gradually transferring the "excess" profits secured through the solidarity policy of wage restraint in centralized collective bargaining into wage-earner or community funds that would eventually have *majority* ownership of all corporations with over twenty-five employees. But in fact, it was not only fought tooth and nail by Swedish capital, but also resisted by Palme's Social Democratic government, which contended it had a fatal flaw: if the transfer of ownership is to be announced and highly gradual, why would owners, knowing there is a timetable for their expropriation, continue to invest? "The capitalists understandably disliked this idea," as Meidner later put it in the 1993 *Socialist Register*. Impressive and ambitious though it was by today's standards, in retrospect it can be understood as an unsuccessful response to the *retreat* of social democratic forces in the face of what Meidner himself had recognized by the late 1960s was part and parcel of "the internationalization of the Swedish economy."[13]

This points to the contradictions of "fund socialism." As experience with the expansion of worker pension funds in financial markets generally shows, far from becoming a form of "labor's capital" and democratizing investment as some had hoped, these funds have served as a major lever for concentrating power in the financial sector and increasing pressure on nonfinancial corporations to maximize "shareholder value." As a result, together with the growth of mutual funds, large institutional investors came to either manage or own directly vast concentrations of corporate shares by the 1980s. That the big public-sector funds often pushed the neoliberal restructuring of these corporations raises serious doubts about the wisdom of identifying "socialism" with the creation of financial market funds managed either by the capitalist state or the trustees of union pension funds. In to-day's intensely competitive global markets, there is little reason to expect worker ownership funds to effect a major—or any—transformation in corporate strategy.

Similar shortcomings are reflected in proposals to extend considerable state support for the formation of worker cooperatives—particularly in the case of plants and facilities that capital has decided to abandon. Taking over facilities that capital doesn't want and trying to run them competitively is worthy of support when desperate workers see it as their only alternative, but this cannot be a strategic foundation for democratizing the economy (and without the most comprehensive supports, may become an example of "lemon socialism" and even discredit the effectiveness of worker democracy). External pressures and internal dynamics can reduce co-ops to sites for achieving a different personal lifestyle or simply operating like another business, if perhaps a more egalitarian one. In the worst case, transferring such uncompetitive firms to worker-owners may help *facilitate* capital's exit from these assets. Unless worker co-ops are part of a social movement looking to larger changes—committing a portion of their revenues and energies to political education and class organizing—their *socialist* impact will be marginal.[14]

Similar challenges would need to be put to consumer and credit cooperatives, which are broadly identified with the left, but whose primarily narrow economic activities need to be politicized—above all in the sense of opening their spaces to radical education about the capitalist context in which they operate, actively participating in left campaigns, and contributing a portion of their revenue to fund organizers to carry out such tasks. Another challenge faces the environmental movement. Workers' defensive prioritization of their jobs is not likely to be effectively countered by speaking to them only in the vague terms of "just transitions" to a clean energy economy. Only by directly engaging with their defensive struggles will it be possible to win committed working class support for the need for democratic control of investment decisions and economic planning so central to finding solutions to the interlinked environmental and socio-economic crises of our times.

The fundamental problem with so many of the current plans for economic democracy is not that they fall short in the proportion of board members or shares allocated to workers, but in the goals themselves. They all tend toward reviving at the firm level a competitive corporatism, whereby workers collaborate with management to enhance the competitiveness of "their" firm against others. And that in turn reproduces pressures internal to the firm to establish hierarchies that aid competitiveness, rather than develop work

relationships that stress equal status and the broadest participation. Democratization can't occur without changing the
context within which economic units, and thus workers, relate to each other—and it is difficult to see strategies whose
horizons are limited to ownership or management of capital
by particular groups of workers in a market economy as a step
toward socialism.

Moreover, while the emphasis on policies to democratize
corporate governance is driven by the more general concern of democratizing the economy, the focus of these reforms underestimates the potential of those democratizing
workplaces that stand, to some degree at least, outside the
competitive discipline of profits and competition. So, for
example, the commitment to expanding the universal provision of basic social services also opens, or should open, a
wide-ranging discussion on how state and para-state agencies in education, health, and social services—where almost
twice as many people work as in manufacturing, and where
there is a degree of autonomy from market pressures—
might be democratically run. To the extent that hierarchies
are eroded for workers in these sectors, and to the extent
that new institutional relationships are established between
public-sector workers providing these services and the people they serve, examples of alternatives to capitalist relationships and practices are concretized and enthusiasm for their
extension can be generated. There are of course pressures
and assumptions other than directly competitive ones that
limit the democratization of publicly owned companies and

state agencies, but deepening workplace democracy in these spaces is a critical opportunity to show what deprivatization can do. And confronting the inherent challenges of how to balance national, regional, local, and workplace goals and democratic practices at this modest scale is clearly critical to developing understandings and capacities for moving to larger scales of economic coordination and collective control.

6

PLANNING FOR
DEMOCRATIC SOCIALISM

A socialist strategy should see economic democracy not just in terms of empowering workers within firms, but of engaging in a political struggle to transform the *conditions* within which productive units operate and how they relate to each other. This requires undertaking a class-based rather than a firm-based struggle for democracy, whereby production is oriented to serving social needs rather than corporate interests. Building the democratic capacities of the working class does not revolve around integrating workers more deeply within capitalist finance or corporate structures in the hope of organizational efficiencies, but rather lies in struggling to replace capitalist competition at the national and international levels with solidaristic democratic planning. Worker representation on company boards and cooperatives could play a role here if leveraged into planning agreements across firms and sectors that aim to fulfill specific democratically determined objectives—for instance, carrying out a green transition. This would have to be supported by a broader plan, coordinated by the state, to advance the democratic control of investment at national and regional levels of the economy.

Any gradual measures to increase worker "voice" by expanding legal ownership or representation within corporate governance must be backed by structural reforms that extend control over capital assets at the point of production through building state planning capacities. Rather than gearing reforms toward competitiveness, workers and communities could fight to extend social control over production, short of outright seizure of control over capital assets, in each of the three areas discussed as follows: 1) cooperative production could be locally coordinated and planned, supported by the national state, such that it is not limited to worker ownership of firms producing competitively for the market; 2) national and regional democratic planning structures could be developed to coordinate the extension of universal basic services (housing, education, parks, day cares); and 3) planning agreements could be implemented among major corporations, leveraged across sectors, with national plans linking planning undertaken by workers within individual firms.

In both the US and UK, the proposals for extending economic democracy have in fact been linked with plans for new mechanisms for increasing and expanding long-term public control and planning of investment. Importantly, these proposals transcend some of the limits of firm-level democracy in seeking to deploy the political agency of the state to determine investment priorities across society as a whole. This involves constructing new state capacities to undertake economic planning in order to break with neoliberal stagnation, reverse deindustrialization and regional inequities, boost employment and wages, and address the climate crisis. In the US, this orientation has revolved around the call for a "Green New Deal," most prominently articulated by Alexandria Ocasio-Cortez since she was elected to Congress. The Green New Deal also formed the basis for the ambitious environmental plan Sanders released for the 2020 Democratic primary. In the UK, Corbyn and McDonnell have advanced plans for a "green industrial revolution" as a component of an industrial strategy that includes a new role for the Bank of England in supervising private investment. Insofar as these plans are presented in the context of a socialist discourse oriented to fundamentally transforming and democratizing the economy, it is important to understand whether, and in what ways, they constitute meaningful steps toward replacing the power of capitalist finance over investment with solidaristic democratic planning, capable of overcoming competitive pressures for profit-driven production.

The ambition of these strategies is constrained by the weakness of the labor movement as well as by the much-reduced capacities of state institutions through four decades of neoliberal restructuring. Moreover, extending democratic control over the economy means confronting the central state economic policy apparatuses that were empowered through these same processes of restructuring, and are today the key seats of control for the dominant sectors of capitalist classes. Orienting them to a radically different agenda will require significant conflict, institutional reorganization, and strategic planning. This challenge is reflected in how each of the above proposals has generally been articulated as a *supplement* to, and not a *replacement* for, private investment and capitalist financial institutions. To assess whether, while operating on the margins of the structures of financialized neoliberal capitalism, such proposals could form part of a strategy for a broader project of democratizing the state and the economy, it may be useful once again to examine them alongside the explicitly non-socialist proposals put forward in the US context by Elizabeth Warren.

Warren's emphasis on strengthening US capitalism through public investment, and cultivation of alliances between popular forces and sections of capital to this end, makes her claims to channel Roosevelt rather more convincing than those democratic socialists who invoke FDR. Warren's "Plan for Economic Patriotism" aims to rejuvenate the US economy through a market-focused state industrial policy to enhance national technology-based competitiveness. In her words, "economic patriotism is about using all the tools we have to boost American workers and American industries so they have the best opportunity to compete internationally."[1] As its title suggests, Warren's plan tries to bridge Trump's economic nationalism and Sanders's democratic socialism.[2] Unlike Trump, Warren rejects blaming globalization or immigration for the suffering caused by neoliberalism; like Sanders, she roots popular frustrations in criticisms of corporations, in particular the financial sector.

The trouble for Warren is that giant corporations "wave the flag—but they have no loyalty or allegiance to America,"

as evidenced by their relocation of production to places like
Mexico and China. Rather than catering to the financial
interests of such disloyal multinationals, she proposes that
"our government do what other leading nations do and act
aggressively" to achieve "faster growth, stronger American industry, and more good American jobs." This includes
counteracting the role of "foreign investors" in driving up
"the value of our currency for their own benefit"; boosting
R&D expenditure while requiring that the resulting production be carried out in the US and distributed equitably across
regions; using government procurements to encourage production within the US; increasing export subsidies through
the Export-Import Bank while requiring it to "focus more
on smaller and medium-sized businesses"; and expanding
worker training programs.[3]

Warren asserts that unlike other states—including China,
Japan, and Germany—the US lacks a centralized industrial
policy, with R&D programs fragmented across myriad state
agencies. A new Department of Economic Development,
which would replace the Commerce Department, would
consolidate these efforts and develop a single, coherent,
market-oriented industrial strategy. That this agency would
also subsume the Office of the US Trade Representative
reflects Warren's concern that over the neoliberal period,
the power and autonomy of state agencies promoting the
internationalization of capital have been consistently en-
hanced.[4] In Warren's terms, this amounts to the empower-
ment of "government agencies that undermine sustainable

American jobs." By consolidating these programs and offices "in one place," she hopes "to make it clear that the unified mission of the federal government is to promote sustainable, middle-class American jobs." Her plan thus seeks to counteract financial short-termism by building the capacity within the state to systematically undertake long-term investment planning. A four-year plan called a "National Jobs Strategy" would "guide how the Department of Economic Development prioritizes its investments and direct its programs," enticing corporations to invest at home by offering subsidies for R&D and up-skilling labor to perform high-value-added production.

This approach has real and immediate limits, based as it is on continuously competing to supply capital with a favorable "investment climate" in which to competitively produce high-value-added exports. As summarized in *National Review*, "Senator Warren's 'economic patriotism' consists of calling the bosses at the Fortune 500 a★★holes and then writing them a check for tens of billions of dollars. I suspect the gentlemen in pinstripes will find a way to endure the insult."[5]

Moreover, Warren's decidedly scaled-down embrace of the Green New Deal proposed by Ocasio-Cortez and supported by Sanders has taken the form of a "Green Manufacturing Plan" that draws on the experience of the industrial mobilization for World War II and the subsequent "space race." The plan calls for addressing the climate crisis through massive state investment—$2 trillion by her estimates—to support the development of new technologies that can then be commodified and sold by manufacturing corporations. As Warren sees it, "over the next decade, the expected market for clean energy technology in emerging economies alone is $23 trillion. America should dominate this new market."[6] In addition to helping ease the US balance of payments by boosting exports, she claims this plan would generate over one million new jobs for "American workers" while targeting investments to reduce regional inequalities.

The Green New Deal introduced in the House of Representatives by Ocasio-Cortez was significantly broader and more ambitious in its intentions.[7] The fourteen-page nonbinding resolution called for a "ten-year national mobilization" to address the climate crisis by "meeting 100 percent of the power demand in the United States through clean, renewable, and zero-emission energy sources"; repairing and upgrading existing infrastructure while constructing new "green" infrastructure, including "smart" power grids; "upgrading all existing buildings in the United States and building new buildings to achieve maximal energy efficiency"; "overhauling transportation systems," including building zero-emission vehicle infrastructure and expanding public transportation and high-speed rail; and "spurring massive growth in clean manufacturing." It also included a host of radical measures such as a federal government job guarantee ("with a family-sustaining wage, adequate family and medical leave, paid vacations, and retirement security") for everyone in the country, as well as "high-quality health care"; "affordable, safe, and adequate housing"; "access to clean water, clean air, healthy and affordable food, and nature"; and "training and high-quality education, including higher education."

Clearly, beyond the urgent call for doing something dramatic, the actual form a GND would ultimately take would be conditioned by significant class and intraclass struggles. While some firms stand to benefit from such a program, large sections of capital will remain vehemently opposed to a GND, which not only jeopardizes the bottom lines of individual corporations (in the case of the extractive sector, possible expropriation), but also threatens to embolden the left and permanently extend a degree of state planning. Yet while the GND and its socialist proponents have taken a directly confrontational approach to business and explicitly emphasized the need for working-class mobilization, the state lacks the administrative, technical, and fiscal capacities to produce and install the technologies and infrastructures required. This means that private capital will likely be involved—and expect a profit—no matter what version of the GND (if any) is implemented. On the other hand, Warren's entire model of "responsible capitalism" rests on the emergence of an alliance between popular forces and a section of capital ready to accept stronger state regulation, direction of investment, and redistribution of income.

The push for a GND has created a significant opening for the left to directly challenge the fossil fuel industry, to link climate change to the broader injustices produced by capitalism, and to identify *both* parties' reliance on corporate financing as being responsible for their joint failure to address the problem. Sanders especially has emphasized the need for working-class people to mobilize against corporate power in the fight for climate justice:

> These companies lied to the American people about the very existence of climate change and committed one of the greatest frauds in the history of our country. Just as the tobacco industry was ultimately forced to pay for the fraud they committed, the fossil fuel industry must be forced to do the same .... We've got an enormous amount of work in front of us. We've got to educate. We've got to organize. And we've got to fight for political power.[8]

The point of such socialist discourse is to stress that, rather than technological policy fixes to deal with the environmental crisis in ways that strengthen capital, the key objective is to find ways to weaken the power of corporations over working-class lives and challenge the logic of competitiveness and profitability. This was in fact the most important aspect of Sanders's own Green New Deal platform announced in August 2019,[9] which not only "ventured into territory rarely touched by presidential candidates [in terms of measures] to facilitate organizing around environmental justice," but whose proposals

> went beyond the fossil fuel industry to point a finger at the broader system of private utilities and public agencies colluding to block renewables and prop up dirty fuels. His plan proposes creating new agencies to produce and

distribute publicly owned clean power on the model of
the original New Deal's Tennessee Valley Authority. And
his plan would encourage the formation of "municipally
and cooperatively owned utilities with democratic, public ownership," providing financing to communities that
want to take literal and figurative power back from inves-
tor-owned electric companies in their own backyards.[10]

For socialists, the principal failures of capitalism are its de-
structive impacts on people's lives and potentials and on
planetary survival, pointing to the need to fight for a radically different way of organizing how we live and relate to
nature. In the context of a GND, this means finding ways
to extend solidaristic democratic planning alongside measures to limit corporate control of intellectual property
and push for the free transfer of green technologies to other societies (rather than via export sales), while identifying
capitalism itself as the problem. Notably John McDonnell's
proposals for dealing with the climate crisis in the UK revealed the extent to which his strategic thinking on these
questions surpassed that of his counterparts in the US. After praising the "Extinction Rebellion" protestors and even
inviting them to brief his policy team, McDonnell pledged
support for a "Sustainable Investment Board" comprised of
the chancellor, business secretary, and Bank of England gov-
ernor to oversee private investment and ensure compliance
with the government's environmental standards and direc-
tives, with the goal of achieving net zero carbon emissions
by 2050. This would be a potentially highly important step

in democratizing the central bank, forcing it to serve social and ecological needs, and gearing its oversight of private investment toward enforcing social priorities beyond merely limiting financial market volatility. In order to enforce these priorities on private investors, McDonnell raised the idea that Labour would delist from the London Stock Exchange those companies that fail to meet environmental standards. The City of London reacted with predictable shock and horror to the proposal, referring to it as "financial totalitarianism" that "could undermine the entire financial system."[11] Yet the proposal highlighted the limitations on the policy options of nation-states in a world of global financial integration—and the importance for socialist strategy of imposing limits on the free movement of capital.[12]

By contrast, while they have called for Congress to spend trillions on infrastructure (green and otherwise), Sanders and Ocasio-Cortez have not, in fact, advanced a specific strategy for transcending Warren's focus on competitiveness, profitability, and commodification. Policies for expanding state investment and using procurement and other regulations to ensure corporate investment occurs at home may have a role, but only as a first step in asserting broader and deeper popular sovereignty over the economy, whereby democratically determined social priorities, rather than the endless accumulation of abstract value, guide investment decisions.

Though the independence such initiatives could have from the forces of capitalist competition should not be exaggerated, they could also have a modicum of protection from capital outflow by virtue of their insulation from financial markets and the pressures of private accumulation, as well as their new popular mandate. The autonomy from capital secured in these spaces could then be used to validate the benefits and possibilities of social ownership—running workplaces in a far more democratic manner and balancing the needs of the workers and communities most involved with broader societal interests. But as vital as such reforms could be, what cannot be set aside is how they would relate to developing greater working-class coherence and confidence—what needs to be seen today in terms of the *remaking* of the working class—to the end of facilitating its commitment to sustaining a long-term socialist strategy.

CONCLUSION:
THE SOCIALIST CHALLENGE TODAY

The profound political dilemma this book has tried to confront is this: for a socialist-led government in the current conjuncture, giant steps toward transformative change would be impossible, but small steps risk being swallowed into the logic of the system. Even meeting the first condition for building on electoral success—i.e., immediately delivering material gains for the working classes—entails being honest about the obstacles in the way. Taxing the 1 percent—or the top 5 or 10 percent—is a good idea for all kinds of obvious reasons. The potential gains from undertaxed and untaxed corporate and financial income and assets, not to mention personal wealth taxes, inheritance taxes, luxury taxes, and so forth, are enormous. But the capacity to do this without effective capital controls needs to be faced squarely. Moreover, the idea that taxing the "billionaire class" would be sufficient to pay for the impressive range of policies proposed by socialists today is clearly fanciful—and tends to underestimate the need for weaning the working class itself away from the anti-tax propaganda of the neoliberal era.

In addition to taxation, state borrowing through the issuance of bonds can finance short-term spending. But as a long-term mechanism for raising indefinite sums, it is constrained by the interest payments these bonds must pay to creditors (generally those with higher incomes), and it leaves social programs vulnerable to financial markets or central banks raising interest rates. Dipping into the very large pools of bargained pension funds is another alternative bandied about, but the particular workers whose deferred wages were placed in these funds will not take kindly to what they will see as their paying for universal benefits without the same earned returns as that on similar assets. At a minimum, the pool would have to be supplemented by a levy on every financial institution (not just pension funds, but also banks and insurance companies). Similarly, "quantitative easing for the many" through relying on central bank powers to issue money credit sounds attractive, but avoids the hard questions of what is entailed in changing the structures and functions of central banking, let alone the constraints that international financial markets would impose through the impact on exchange rates and the outflow of capital.[1]

An overriding limit in all the steps toward taking control over economic life, even in the case of relatively modest expansions of social provision, is the power of capital to exit and invest abroad (along with the refusal of capital to keep coming in). Overcoming that threat and getting control over the funds to complete the socialist project must, at some point, raise the necessity of imposing controls on finance. It is, however, critical to see this not as merely "keeping capital at home" along the lines of "economic patriotism." If such controls are to be meaningful, they must extend to *what happens to this capital* even if it is forced to remain.

This is where the second condition for building on any socialist electoral successes comes in, requiring the opening of new paths to structural reform through expanding economic democracy, public investment, and—critically—economic planning. There is no escaping the fact that radically different priorities imply not just a redistribution of income and control over money, but a real redistribution of how society's labor, equipment, and resources are used, and to what ends. And we must be fully aware that this redistribution not only involves severe impositions on capital, but also includes a cultural shift within the working class from individual consumption to greater collective consumption. Such a transformation would have to occur alongside the development of new political capacities, whereby workers go beyond expanding their control of "their" workplaces to extending democratic control of the economy. The limits we have identified in current proposals for economic democracy and investment planning reflect the limited abilities of working classes to struggle for broader and deeper reforms.

Though the "Green New Deal" and "just transitions" for working people have become central parts of the lexicon of today's socialist discourse, these well-intentioned calls to action and promises of secure transitions remain, for "the many," mostly abstract slogans, reflecting the distance between policy and grounded participation. Yet the dynamics of capitalist restructuring create new possibilities for linking the need to address the environmental crisis with practical and immediate struggles. Identifying the regular drumbeat of closures as a loss of essential collective productive capacities raises the possibility of socializing and converting these facilities to the production of "green" products and infrastructure. The point of such conversions would be to combine workers' skills with the equipment capital has rejected to manufacture products of social and ecological value.

Working-class mobilizations at the community and plant levels could be linked to the initiatives of a socialist-led government to institutionalize a wide range of supports led by a new "public conversion agency." Placing abandoned facilities and equipment in the public domain rather than leaving them to groups of workers "owning" their workplaces would allow for the establishment of research units in each community or region staffed by working teams engaged in exploring both the technical and social dimensions of conversion, with higher environmental standards in turn increasing the demand for "green" goods. Local conversion councils would take on the task of developing environmental/industrial literacy and strengthening community engagement. And as such capacities develop, the facilities targeted could extend from those that corporations no longer want to new or existing facilities that can make critical contributions to addressing the environmental crisis, and eventually—and organically—to taking on the "commanding heights" of the economy. What is central here is the link between concrete everyday struggles in communities with the politics of environmental transformation.

What would need to be strategically addressed, first of all, by a socialist-led government would be how to most constructively transform public institutions—not only so as to render them capable of fully supporting such reforms, but to simultaneously continue to build a politically coherent working class. In other words, the key strategic challenge would be to link policies of reform to the development of the sorts of state and class capacities that together could realize socialist possibilities. This requires moving beyond alternative policies to an alternative *politics* concerned with developing worker and community solidarity, strategic coherence, and socialist commitments reflected in a growing popular self-assurance to push ahead.

By the beginning of the twenty-first century, aided by the realization of a fully global capitalism and the networked structures of production, finance, and consumption that constitute it, there were more workers on the face of the Earth than ever before. New technologies certainly restricted job growth in certain sectors, but entirely new sectors in both manufacturing and especially high-tech services had been created. Though these developments weakened the leverage of class struggles in important ways, they also introduced new points of strategic potential: strikes at component plants or interruptions of supplier chains at warehouses and ports could force shutdowns throughout a globally integrated production network, and whistleblowing could expose vast stores of information hidden by corporations and states.

The precarious conditions workers increasingly face today, even when they belong to unions, speak not to a new class division between precariat and proletariat. Precariousness rather reflects how previous processes of working-class formation and organization have become undone. Precariousness is not something new in capitalism: employers have always tried to gain access to labor when they want, dispose of it as they want, and, in between, use it with as few restrictions as possible. There is in this context limited value in drawing new sociological nets of who is or is not in the working class. Rather than categorizing workers into different strata—nurses or baristas, teachers or software developers, farmhands or truckers, salespeople or bank tellers—what needs to preoccupy our imaginations and inform our strategic calculations is how to visualize and develop the potential of new forms of working-class organization and formation in the twenty-first century.

There are indeed multitudes of workers' struggles taking place today in the face of an increasingly exploitative and chaotic capitalism. Yet there is no denying that prospects for working-class transformative agency seem dim. Factors internal to working-class institutions, their contradictions and weaknesses, allowed—in the developing as well as the developed countries—for the passage of free trade, the liberalization of finance, the persistence of austerity, the further commodification of labor power, and the restructuring of all dimensions of economic and social life in today's global capitalism. The inability of the working class to renew itself and discover new organizational forms in light of the dynamism of capital and capacities of the state to contain worker resistance has allowed the far right today to articulate and contextualize a set of common sentiments linked to the crisis—frustrations with insecurity and inequality and anger with parties that once claimed to represent workers' interests. Escaping this crisis of the working class is not primarily a matter of better policies or better tactics. It is primarily an *organizational* challenge to facilitate new processes of class formation rooted in the multiple dimensions of workers' lives that encompass so many identities and communities.

Meeting this challenge would require that a socialist-led government give priority to strengthening unions institutionally. Labor law reforms are being advanced to reestablish and extend legal requirements for union recognition and dues check-off. Sanders has gone so far as to promise that his radical proposals along these lines would double union density in four years.[2] But such state support for restoring union density—as opposed to removing barriers to unions actively organizing new members—raises serious questions about the *kind* of unionism that will emerge. Numerically stronger unions will indeed be critical to sustain the most significant policy initiatives of any socialist-led government. But the expansion of unions in their present form would not necessarily yield unions oriented to building the class and advancing socialism, as opposed to making particularistic gains within capitalism. Building the class is not the same as increasing union density. Recognizing this should lead to an emphasis on those kinds of proposals in Sanders's "Workplace Democracy Plan"[3] that advance the kinds of changes that would facilitate working-class formation: easing secondary boycotts

to strengthen solidarity, providing access to corporate information as an alternative to granting workers seats on boards
and thereby compromising class independence, and raising
minimum wages and labor standards for the weakest sections
of the class, not only because it is the egalitarian thing to do,
but also because reducing inequalities within the class is a
condition for easing tensions that stand in the way of unity.

The severely limited internal democratic practices, organizing capacities, and political ambitions of unions today un-
derline what must be a key strategic conclusion: advancing
economic democracy *and* planning also requires substantial
transformations in working-class organizations themselves.
The emergence of new socialist forces in both the Democratic Party and the Labour Party cannot be understood except in
relation to the longstanding linkages between the unions and
these parties, which have been of a kind that has undermined
rather than sustained socialist forces. It is to be hoped, however, that this experience will help lay the groundwork for
finally discovering what kinds of unions and parties can give
coherence to the socialist project in the twenty-first century.

To stress the importance of a democratic socialist strategy
for entering the state through elections to the end of transforming the state is today, less than ever, a matter of discovering a smooth gradual road to socialism. Reversals, of various
intensities, are inescapable. Governments reaching beyond
capitalism will never have the luxury of "circumstances they
choose for themselves."[4] Moreover, the basic problem for any
government oriented to pursuing a socialist project is that

the very challenge to capital's hegemony will likely spark, or aggravate, an economic crisis that will make it difficult to satisfy popular expectations for the promised relief from inequality and austerity. How to cope with this while not pushing off to an indefinite future the measures needed to begin the transformation of the state is the crucial socialist political challenge.

It is this tension among the various new state responsibilities that makes the role of socialist parties that will bring such governments to office so fundamental. Given the legitimacy and resources that inevitably will accrue to those party leaders who form the government, the autonomy of the party, which must more than ever keep its feet in the movements, is necessary in order to counter the pull from inside the state toward social democratization. This is why strategic preparations undertaken well before entering the state to avoid replicating the experience with social democracy are so very important. But even given such readiness, the process of transforming the state cannot help but be complex, uncertain, and crisis-ridden, with repeated interruptions. Transformations of state apparatuses at local or regional levels where circumstances and the balance of forces are more favorable may be more successfully pursued, including developing alternative means of producing and distributing food, health care, and other necessities at community levels. This could have the further benefit of facilitating and encouraging the involvement of many traditionally marginalized groups as well as stimulate autonomous movements moving in these directions through takeovers of land, idle buildings, threatened factories, and transportation networks. All this progress may in turn spur developments at the higher levels of state power, ranging over time from codifying new collective property rights to developing and coordinating agencies of democratic planning. At some points in this process, more or less dramatic initiatives of nationalization and socialization of industry and finance would have to take place, being careful to "mind the gap" between participatory socialist politics and previous versions of state ownership.

Given how state apparatuses are now structured so as to reproduce capitalist social relations, their institutional modalities would need to undergo fundamental transformations. Public employees would themselves need to become explicit agents of transformation, aided and sustained in this respect by their unions and the broader labor movement. Rather than expressing defensive particularism, unions themselves would need to be changed fundamentally so they can actively engage in developing state workers' transformational capacities, including by establishing councils that link them to the recipients of state services.

The broad point here is that reform versus revolution is not a useful way to frame the dilemmas that socialists must confront today. Political hopes are inseparable from notions of what is possible. And possibility is itself intimately related to working-class formation—and indeed *reformation* of the broadest possible kind—and the role of socialist parties in that formation. Getting socialism seriously on the agenda requires addressing the question of political agency more broadly and deeply to include developing that agency's capacity for state transformation so that governments with a socialist project not be stymied by the inherited state apparatuses. In this respect, socialist parties in the twenty-first century must not see themselves as a kind of omnipotent deus ex machina. Precisely in order not to draw back from the "prodigious scope of their own aims," as Marx once put it, they must "engage in perpetual self-criticism" and deride "the inadequacies, weak points, and pitiful aspects of their first attempts."[5]

NOTES

Chapter 1: The Revival of Democratic Socialism

1. See Leo Panitch and Colin Leys, *The End of Parliamentary Socialism: From New Left to New Labour*, 2nd ed. (London: Verso, 2001), Chs. 3 and 4 passim, and Ch. 6, 118–24, and the forthcoming *Searching for Socialism: The Project of the New Labour Left from Benn to Corbyn* (London: Verso, 2020).

2. As *The Communist Manifesto* put it, in elaborating on the bourgeoisie's "highly revolutionary role" historically, "the bourgeoisie cannot exist without constantly revolutionizing the instruments of production, and thereby relations of production, and with them the whole relations of society . . . . In a phrase, it creates a world in its own image." See Karl Marx, *Later Political Writings*, edited and translated by Terrell Carver (Cambridge, UK: Cambridge University Press, 1996), 3–5. For a discussion of the continuing implications of this, see Leo Panitch, "Capitalism, Socialism and Revolution," in Ralph Miliband, Leo Panitch, and John Saville, eds., *The Socialist Register 1989* (London: Merlin Press, 1989); and *Renewing Socialism: Transforming Democracy, Strategy and Imagination,* (London: Merlin Press, 2009).

3. Between the 1987 American stock market crash and the investment banking collapse two decades later, there were upwards of a hundred distinct currency and banking crises as a direct outcome of global capital mobility. States were no longer in the business of "crisis prevention" through regulations that might impede the free flow of capital; rather they were in the business of "crisis containment," as the US Treasury itself put it in explaining why its central role had become "firefighting." See Leo Panitch and Sam Gindin, *The Making of Global Capitalism: The Political Economy of American Empire* (London: Verso, 2012), Chs. 10–2.

4. Perry Anderson, "Renewals," *New Left Review* 1, January/February (2000): 7, 13. "Whatever limitations persist to its practice, neoliberalism as a set of principles rules undivided across the globe: the most successful ideology in world history."

5.   Andrew Murray, "Jeremy Corbyn and the Battle for Socialism," *Jacobin* 7, February (2016).

6.   Jodi Dean, *Crowds and Party* (London: Verso, 2016), 10.

Chapter 2: Class, Party, State:
The Twentieth-Century Socialist Experience

1.   Marx, *Later Political Writings*, 9–0.

2.   See E.P. Thompson, *The Making of the English Working Class* (New York: Pantheon, 1964), 9–1; and "Eighteenth Century English Society: Class Struggle Without Class," *Social History* 3, no. 2, (1978): 133–65.

3.   E. H. Hobsbawm, "The Making of the Working Class, 1870–1914," in *Uncommon People: Resistance, Rebellion and Jazz* (New York: The New Press, 1999) 58–9. See also Geoff Eley, *Forging Democracy: The History of the Left in Europe, 1850–2000* (New York: Oxford University Press, 2002).

4.   Robert Michels, *Political Parties: A Sociological Study of the Oligarchical Tendencies of Modern Democracy* (New York: Free Press, 1962).

5.   Rosa Luxemburg, "The Russian Revolution," in Peter Hudis and Kevin Anderson, eds., *The Rosa Luxemburg Reader* (New York: Monthly Review Press, 2004), 304–6.

6.   Isaac Deutscher, *The Prophet Armed* (London: Oxford University Press, 1954), 505–6.

7.   Quoted in L. Panitch and S. Gindin, "Moscow, Togliatti, Yaroslavl: Perspectives on Perestroika," in Dan Benedict et al., eds., *Canadians Look at Soviet Auto Workers' Unions* (Toronto: CAW, 1992), 19.

8.   "An American Proposal," *Fortune*, May 1942. See also Panitch and Gindin, *The Making*, 67–68.

9.   See Leo Panitch, "Socialist Renewal and the Labour Party," *Socialist Register 1988*, 319–65.

10.   André Gorz, "Reform and Revolution," in Ralph Miliband and John Saville, eds., *The Socialist Register 1968* (London: Merlin Press, 1968); Lucio Magri, "Problems of the Marxist Theory of the Revolutionary Party," *New Left Review* 60, March/April (1970); Tony Benn, *The New Politics: A Socialist Reconnaissance*, Fabian Tract 402, September (1970); Ralph Miliband, "Moving On," in Ralph Miliband and John Saville, eds., *The Socialist Register 1976* (London: Merlin Press, 1976); Ralph

Miliband, *Marxism and Politics* (Oxford: Oxford University Press, 1977); and Sheila Rowbotham, Lynne Segal, and Hilary Wainwright, *Beyond the Fragments: Feminism and the Making of Socialism* (London: Merlin Press, 1979).

11.   Nicos Poulantzas, "Toward a Democratic Socialism," in *State, Power, Socialism* (London: NLB, 1978). The quotes that follow are drawn from pp. 256–261.

12.   Gorz, "Reform and Revolution," 112.

13.   Gorz, "Reform and Revolution," 132–33. Lucio Magri ("Problems of the Marxist Theory of the Revolutionary Party," 128) similarly called for new workers' councils "right across society (factories, offices, schools), with their own structures as mediating organizations between party, union, and state institutions, for which all of the latter needed to act as elements of stimulus and synthesis." And even though he presented this call in terms of the "need for a creative revival of the theme of *soviets* [as] essential to resolve the theoretical and strategic problems of the Western Revolution," his idea was directed at offsetting the total dominance of the party, and emphatically did not mean reendorsing a dual power strategy for smashing the state.

14.   Poulantzas, "Toward a Democratic Socialism," 256, 258.

15.   Ralph Miliband, *Class Power and State Power* (London: Verso, 1983), esp. Chs. 2–4.

16.   Göran Therborn, *What Does the Ruling Class Do When it Rules? State Apparatuses and State Power under Feudalism, Capitalism and Socialism* (London: NLB, 1978), 279–80.

17.   See, however, Greg Albo, David Langille, and Leo Panitch, eds., *A Different Kind of State: Popular Power and Democratic Administration* (Toronto: OUP, 1993).

18.   Sam Gindin, "Chasing Utopia," *Jacobin* 10, March (2016).

19.   Poulantzas, "Toward a Democratic Socialism," 262.

Chapter 3: From Protest to Party to State: Lessons from Syriza

1.   Costas Eleftheriou, "The Uneasy 'Symbiosis': Factionalism and Radical Politics in Synaspismos," paper prepared for The 4th Hellenic Observatory PhD Symposium (n.d.).

2. Michalis Spourdalakis, "Left Strategy in the Greek Cauldron: Explaining Syriza's Success," in Leo Panitch, Greg Albo, and Vivek Chibber, eds., *Socialist Register 2013: The Question of Strategy* (London: Merlin Press, 2012), 102.

3. Available at .https://left.gr/news/political-resolution-1st-congress -SYRIZA.

4. "Syriza and Socialist Strategy," *International Socialism* 146, April (2015) (transcript of a debate between Alec Callinicos and Stathis Kouvelakis, London, February 25, 2015).

5. Costas Douzinas, "The Left in Power? Notes on Syriza's Rise, Fall and (Possible) Second Rise," Near Futures Online, March 2016, http:// nearfuturesonline.org.

6. For the perspective of those who remained in Syriza in the hope of reviving the party outside government as the key agent of transformation, see Michalis Spourdalakis, "Becoming Syriza Again," *Jacobin* 31, January (2016).

7. Andreas Karitzis, *The European Left in Times of Crises: Lessons from Greece* (Amsterdam: Transnational Institute, 2017), 30.

8. Karitzis, *The European Left,* 30–32.

9. Ibid., 20–21.

10. Ibid., 23–24.

11. www.solidarity4all.gr/; https://www.greenleft.org.au/content/greece -solidarity-action-visit-solidarity4all-clinic.

Chapter 4: Corbyn's Challenge:
From Party Insurgency to State Transformation?

1. Ralph Miliband, "Moving On," in Ralph Miliband and John Saville, eds., *The Socialist Register 1976* (London: Merlin Press, 1976), 128, 138.

2. See Andrew Murray's sharp critique of the Left Unity initiative, "Left Unity or Class Unity? Working-class politics in Britain," in Leo Panitch, Greg Albo, and Vivek Chibber, *Registering Class: Socialist Register 2014* (London: Merlin Press, 2013). Murray himself could hardly have imagined then that only three years later he would be seconded from his position as chief of staff of Unite, Britain largest union, to the Labour party leader's election campaign office.

3.   Tony Benn, "Democratic Politics," Fabian Autumn Lecture, November 3, 1971, in *Speeches by Tony Benn*, 277–79; and Tony Benn, *The New Politics: A Socialist Reconnaissance*. See also "Tony Benn: Articulating a New Socialist Politics," in Panitch and Leys, *The End of Parliamentary Socialism*, Ch. 3.

4.   Alex Nunns, *The Candidate: Jeremy Corbyn's Improbable Path to Power*, (London: OR Books, 2018), 147.

5.   Richard Seymour, *Corbyn: The Strange Rebirth of Radical Politics* (London: Verso, 2017), 174.

6.   Nunns, *The Candidate*, 147.

7.   Tom Blackburn, "Corbynism from Below," New Socialist, June 12, 2017, https://newsocialist.org.uk/corbynism-from-below/.

8.   https://labour.org.uk/about/democracy-review-2017/.

9.   Max Shanly, "Toward a New Model Young Labour," The Bullet, November 27, 2017, https://socialistproject.ca/2017/11/b1516/.

10.   See Panitch and Leys, *The End of Parliamentary Socialism,* esp. Ch. 8.

11.   *For the Many, Not the Few.* https://labour.org.uk/manifesto/.

12.   "Alternative Models of Ownership," Report to the Shadow Chancellor of the Exchequer and Shadow Secretary of State for Business, Energy, and Industrial Strategy, https://labour.org.uk/wp-content/uploads /2017/10/Alternative-Models-of-Ownership.pdf.

13.   John McDonnell, speech at Alternative Models of Ownership conference, London, February 10, 2018, available at: www.john-mcdonnell. net/john_s_speech. The way this speech was reported in the mainstream media illustrates the extreme difficulty faced by the Labour leadership in getting heard. The only "broadsheet" to give it reasonable coverage was the (online) *Independent*. The BBC's coverage was minimal and negative: "John McDonnell: Labour public ownership plan will cost nothing," BBC, February 10, 2018.

14.   John McDonnell, speech to Labour Party Conference, September 24, 2018.

15.   In some ways, it is less desirable than a conventional tax, since corporations are able to decide on the level of dividends they pay out—and thus their contribution to this flexible "tax."

16.   Hilary Wainwright, *A New Politics from the Left*, (Cambridge, UK: Polity, 2018).

17.   Paul Mason, *Post-Capitalism* (London: Allen Lane, 2015).

18.   Quoted in Panitch and Leys, *The End of Parliamentary Socialism*, 174–75.

19.   Nicholas Costello, Jonathan Michie, and Seumas Milne, *Beyond the Casino Economy* (London: Verso, 1989), 254–25.

20.   Nina Power, "Digital Democracy," in L. Panitch and G. Albo, eds., *Rethinking Democracy: Socialist Register 2018* (London: Merlin Press, 2017), 174.

21.   Jeremy Gilbert, "Leading Richer Lives," in Mike Phipps, ed., *For the Many: Preparing Labour for Power* (London: OR Books, 2017), 175.

22.   For a good overview, see Robin Blackburn, "The Corbyn Project: Public Capital and Labour's New Deal," *New Left Review* 111, May/June (2018): 5–32. See *Labour's Fiscal Credibility Rule* (2017); *Richer Britain, Richer Lives: Labour's Industrial Strategy* (2017); *A National Investment Bank for Britain: Putting Dynamism into our Industrial Strategy* (2017); and *The Green Transformation: Labour's Environment Policy.* (2018), all available at www.labour.org.uk.

23.   Jim Pickard, "John McDonnell interview: is Britain ready for a socialist chancellor?" *Financial Times*, March 2, 2018.

24.   Graham Turner et al., *Financing Investment: Final Report*, GFC Economics and Clearpoint Advisors, June 20, 2018, 102, available at www.labour.org.uk. Although the report was careful to make clear that it did not represent the views of the Labour Party nor the Shadow Chancellor of the Exchequer, it appeared on the Labour Party's website as soon as it was completed. See also Josh Halliday, "Labour would break up Treasury and create northern No 11, says McDonnell," *The Guardian*, July 7, 2019.

25.   The *Financing Investment* report's conception of such enterprises as part of "high-tech clusters" does not begin to address this problem. And although it was praised by McDonnell in his speech to the 2018 party conference, the final report of the IPPR's Commission on Economic Justice (*Prosperity and Justice: A plan for the new economy* [London: IPPR, September 2018]) did not begin to do so either, especially with its notions of "industrial clusters" operating amid "more open and competitive markets" under the rubric of a "partnership economy" between capital, labor, and the state.

26.   Jim Pickard, "Labour plans for capital flight or run on pound if elected," *Financial Times*, September 26, 2017.

27.   Christine Berry and Laurie Macfarlane, "A New Public Banking Ecosystem: A report to the Labour Party commission by the Communication Workers Union and the Democracy Collaborative," (2019).

28. As it has been defined in *Road Map to a Green New Deal: From Extraction to Stewardship* (London: Common Wealth, July 2019), 12. Notably this report traces its roots to the path charted by the original Green New Deal group's first report, *A Green New Deal*, published by the New Economics Foundation (NEF) in 2008.

29. *Land for the Many: Changing the Way Our Fundamental Asset is Used, Owned and Governed*, (London: Labour Party, June 2019), 44, available at labour. org.uk. See André Gorz, "Reform and Revolution," in Ralph Miliband and John Saville, eds., *Socialist Register 1968* (London: Merlin Press, 1967). The Monbiot Report cites Gorz's book of the same year: *Strategy for Labor,* (Boston: Beacon Press, 1968).

30. This is at the root of the argument made by the Foundational Economy Collective. The "providential foundational economy" is defined as comprising mainly public sector (but increasingly outsourced) activities providing universal services, such as health, education, social care, police, and public administration, plus their close private suppliers, while the "material foundational economy" comprises the infrastructure of everyday life, such as pipes and cables providing electricity, gas, water, sewage, and telecommunications to households, in addition to railways, roads, filling stations, and auto services, as well as the public/social vehicles that use them such as buses and trains. Once public postal services and private retail banking (also defined as essential to everyday life) are included, the foundational economy as a whole accounts for almost 44 percent of employment in the UK as well as in Germany, and at least a third in other high-income countries. See *Foundational Economy* (Manchester: Manchester University Press, 2019), 23–24, 40–41.

31. An essential first step in this direction is *Democratising Local Public Services: A Plan for Twenty-First Century Insourcing*, A Labour Party Report, Community Wealth Building Unit 2019. In introducing this report, McDonnell said, "Local government is a key site for building a socialist society, and today is another step on the road to giving local councils the powers they need to contribute to that society . . . . Insourcing is an essential part of a programme for practical socialism, which delivers people's basic needs and improves people's everyday lives." See John McDonnell, speech at the launch of Democratising Local Public Services, July 20, 2019, available at labour.org.uk.

Chapter 5: Sanders's Challenge: Economic Democracy beyond "Responsible Capitalism"?

1. Bernie Sanders, "Prepared Remarks: The Political Revolution Continues." June 16, 2016, https://berniesanders.com/political-revolution-continues.

2. Dan La Botz, "Life After Bernie: People's Summit Searches for the Movement's Political Future," *New Politics,* June 21, 2016, http://newpol.org.

3. See Steve Williams and Rishi Awatramani, "New Working-Class Organizations and the Social Movement Left"; and Mark Dudzic and Adolph Reed, Jr., "The Crisis of Labour and the Left in the United States," both in Leo Panitch and Greg Albo, eds., *Socialist Register 2015: Transforming Classes* (London: Merlin Press, 2014).

4. Eric Blanc, *Red State Revolt: The Teachers' Strike Wave and Working-Class Politics,* (London: Verso, 2019).

5. Matthew Yglesias, "Bernie Sanders's plan to break up the banks, explained," Vox, January 21, 2016.

6. Accountable Capitalism Act, S.3348, 115th United States Congress, 2018.

7. Elizabeth Warren, "Companies Shouldn't Be Accountable Only to Shareholders," *Wall Street Journal,* August 14, 2018.

8. The argument that finance is starving non-financial corporations of funds for investment doesn't tally with the fact that high corporate profits and low interest rates indicate there is no shortage of potential funds. On the other hand, a corollary of the relative dominance of finance within the US and UK is that both economies are skewed not only to finance but to related business services like consultancies, accountants, lawyers, and real estate, and so manufacturing output and employment are a smaller part of their overall economic activity.

9. See Michael Useem, *Executive Defense: Shareholder Power and Corporate Reorganization* (Boston: Harvard University Press, 1993); and Jesse Fried, "Trump and Warren offer the wrong diagnosis of short-termism," *Financial Times,* August 27, 2018.

10. Rachel M. Cohen, "Could Expanding Employee Ownership Be The Next Big Economic Policy?" *The Intercept,* December 26, 2018.

11. Bernie Sanders, Speech at 2018 Vermont Employee Ownership Conference, available at www.youtube.com.

12. Jeff Stein, "Bernie Sanders backs two policies to dramatically shift corporate power to US workers," *Washington Post,* June 20, 2019. See Bernie Sanders,

"Corporate Accountability and Democracy," https://berniesanders.com /issues/corporate-accountability-and-democracy/.

13.   Rudolph Meidner, "Why Did the Swedish Model Fail?," in Ralph Miliband and Leo Panitch, eds., *Socialist Register 1993: Real Problems, False Solutions* (London: Merlin Press, 1993), 217, 225.

14.   Gindin, "Chasing Utopia."

Chapter 6: Planning for Democratic Socialism

1.   Elizabeth Warren, "A Plan For Economic Patriotism," Medium, June 4, 2019, available at www.medium.com.

2.   Warren's strident nationalist rhetoric led hard-right Fox News commentator Tucker Carlson to proclaim "she sounds like Trump at his best." See Isaac Stanley-Becker, "'She sounds like Trump at his best': Tucker Carlson endorses Elizabeth Warren's economic populism," *Washington Post*, June 6, 2019. Daniel Drezner of the Fletcher School in Law and Diplomacy at Tufts has similarly—and with equal exaggeration—characterized Warren's program as "Trumpism with a human face." See "Elizabeth Warren's unusual brand of wonkish populism," *The Economist*, February 2, 2019, 23.

3.   Warren, "A Plan For Economic Patriotism."

4.   As discussed in Panitch and Gindin, *The Making*, Chs. 10 and 11.

5.   Kevin D. Williamson, "Colbert Reports," *National Review*, June 9, 2019.

6.   Elizabeth Warren, "My Green Manufacturing Plan For America," Medium, June 4, 2019, available at www.medium.com. This plan relies on the support of the Department of Economic Development in implementing a "Green Apollo Project" by investing $400 billion over ten years in clean energy development (more than ten times what was invested over the last decade), a $1.5 trillion procurement commitment over ten years to purchase "American-made" clean energy products, expanded export subsidies through the Export-Import Bank, and a "Green Marshall Plan" that entails "a commitment to using all the tools in our diplomatic and economic arsenal to encourage other countries to purchase and deploy American-made clean energy technology."

7.   Recognizing the duty of the Federal Government to create a Green New Deal, H.Res. 109, 116th United States Congress (first session), 2019–2020. See Myron Ebell, "Green New Deal Launched with Support from Democratic Presidential Candidates," Competitive Enterprise

Institute, February 11, 2019; and Rex Santus, "AOC's Green New Deal has the backing of every major 2020 candidate," *Vice*, February 7, 2019.

8. Miranda Green, "Sanders and Ocasio-Cortez join up to preach Green New Deal, take jabs at Biden," The Hill, May 13, 2019.

9. See "The Green New Deal" at https://berniesanders.com/issues/the-green -new-deal/.

10. Alyssa Battistoni and Thea Riofrancos, "Bernie Sanders's Green New Deal Is a Climate Plan for the Many Not the Few," *Jacobin*, August 23, 2019.

11. Owen Bennett, "City voices anger at John McDonnell's 'financial totalitarianism' climate change plans," *City A.M.*, June 25, 2019.

12. Though the importance of the City of London in global financial markets makes the threat to delist companies far from insignificant, the possibility for capitalists to raise capital on other stock exchanges around the world, especially in New York, would mitigate the impact of such a move. In fact, the uniqueness of Wall Street in the global economy suggests that such a strategy could have a more significant impact if implemented in the US—though neither Sanders nor Ocasio-Cortez have gone so far as to suggest anything like this as part of a more general avoidance of directly addressing how to transform the financial system and deal with the power of the Federal Reserve.

Conclusion: The Socialist Challenge Today

1. See the important critiques of such proposals coming from "modern monetary theorists" by Doug Henwood and James Meadway: Doug Henwood, "Modern Monetary Theory Isn't Helping," *Jacobin*, February 21, 2019; James Meadway, "Against MMT," *Tribune*, March 6, 2019.

2. Thomas Kaplan and Noam Scheiber, "Bernie Sets a Plan: Double Union Membership in Four Years," *New York Times*, August 21, 2019, https://www. nytimes.com/2019/08/21/us/politics/2020-democrats-iowa-labor -unions.html.

3. "The Workplace Democracy Plan," https://berniesanders.com/issues/ the-workplace-democracy-plan/.

4. Marx, "The Eighteenth Brumaire of Louis Bonaparte," in *Later Political Writings*, 32.

5. Marx, 35.

ABOUT HAYMARKET BOOKS

Haymarket Books is a radical, independent, nonprofit book publisher based in Chicago.

Our mission is to publish books that contribute to struggles for social and economic justice. We strive to make our books a vibrant and organic part of social movements and the education and development of a critical, engaged, international left.

We take inspiration and courage from our namesakes, the Haymarket martyrs, who gave their lives fighting for a better world. Their 1886 struggle for the eight-hour day—which gave us May Day, the international workers' holiday—reminds workers around the world that ordinary people can organize and struggle for their own liberation. These struggles continue today across the globe—struggles against oppression, exploitation, poverty, and war.

Since our founding in 2001, Haymarket Books has published more than five hundred titles. Radically independent, we seek to drive a wedge into the risk-averse world of corporate book publishing. Our authors include Noam Chomsky, Arundhati Roy, Rebecca Solnit, Angela Y. Davis, Howard Zinn, Amy Goodman, Wallace Shawn, Mike Davis, Winona LaDuke, Ilan Pappé, Richard Wolff, Dave Zirin, Keeanga-Yamahtta Taylor, Nick Turse, Dahr Jamail, David Barsamian, Elizabeth Laird, Amira Hass, Mark Steel, Avi Lewis, Naomi Klein, and Neil Davidson. We are also the trade publishers of the acclaimed Historical Materialism Book Series and of Dispatch Books.